MW00533978

THE GREAT ROAD OF LIFE

BY WAYNE SCHELL

Copyright © 2021 by Wayne Schell. All rights reserved.

Written by: Wayne Schell
Cover by: Dee Hunter
Designed by: Susan Newman-Harrison

All rights reserved. No part of this publication may be reproduced, stored
in a retrieval system, or transmitted in any form or by any means—
electronic, mechanical, photocopying, recording, or otherwise—except
for brief quotations in critical reviews or articles, without the prior written
permission of the publisher and copyright owners.

Library of Congress Control Number: Pending

ISBN 978-1-7337293-6-9

THE GREAT ROAD OF LIFE

BY WAYNE SCHELL

TABLE OF CONTENTS

Dedication 1

Introduction 4

Chapter 1 5

Chapter 2 10

Chapter 3 15

Chapter 4 17

Chapter 5 22

Chapter 6 24

Chapter 7 25

Chapter 8 27

Chapter 9 31

Chapter 10 37

Chapter 11 39

Chapter 12 42

Chapter 13 44

Chapter 14 46

Chapter 15 49

Favorite Photos.. 52

Epilogue 60

About the Author... 61

DEDICATION

I dedicate this book to my wonderful wife and friend for over 40 years, Suzanne. Most people are lucky if they find a life partner who is compatible with more than 50% of what they were seeking in their spouse. I can honestly say, Suzanne exceeds 95% of what I thought a spouse should be. She certainly is the number one factor in my success.

I wrote my autobiography to memorialize my views of life on earth for 85 years now. Hopefully, a few young people starting life without a silver spoon in their mouth will pick-up my book and read it. Hopefully, it will inspire them to strive for what I have achieved and teach them that for the vast majority of us, success does not come easily. Easy success is very rare.

Those who excel in sports or become a movie star overnight or a social media founder are few and far between. It's as rare as winning a lottery. But, if you're sincere, dedicated and yes, a little lucky, you too can make a difference here on earth.

—Wayne Schell

My family in front of the old house we lived in.
I was fourteen (R) and that's my older brother who was in the Airforce in 1951.

INTRODUCTION

Everyone has stories to tell about their road through life. I think mine is one of the more uplifting ones. If I can inspire just one of you to make a difference while you spend your precious moments on earth, then sharing my story was worth the effort. Many people go through life complaining about the bad cards life has dealt them. When they die, they have accomplished very little to make the planet a better place than it was when they arrived. When I die, I think I will have had the satisfaction of knowing that I have made many people smile with my jokes and made many people's lives better for having interacted with me. With that said, please enjoy my Great Road of Life.

Brothers Dick (L) and Wayne (R) Schell

CHAPTER 1

I was born in central Illinois in 1936 in the middle of the great depression. It was July 16 and it was the hottest day in history in Illinois 112° fahrenheit. I was the first child in my family born in a hospital, my brother was born at home three years earlier. The day I was born, my father was driving an ice truck and going down the hill into the Illinois River Valley, and the brakes failed. He had to jump out of the truck to avoid going into the river. He ended up in a hospital bed, beside my mother and me.

My father's mother died giving birth to my father. He was raised by a mean stepmother. In 1929, when he was 16 years old he ran away from home. The stock market crashed that year and it was very difficult for anyone to find a job. He became friends with five brothers and cousins. They, along with my father, became hobos and traveled the country in box cars. It was not an uncommon thing in those days. In 1930, my father and his five new friends arrived in a town called Peru, Illinois. These five young men and my father met my mother, her sister, and their four cousins. Can you believe that all six of them married and became relatives?

In 1931, my father and his five friends all purchased lots on Market Street in Peru side-by-side. Since there was no work, the five of them helped each other build houses. There was a brick factory down the street where the workers would throw away the bricks with chips on them, every day and my father and his friends would go down and wheel barrow and take them to their construction sites. A few blocks south of there was a nail factory, the employees there would do the same. There was a wealthy man that was building houses during the depression, and they struck a deal with him that they would demolish the old homes if they could get the lumber, windows and so forth to build their homes. They were very creative. My Dad couldn't afford the bathroom fixtures at the time, but he set aside a room for the bathroom room anyway. The old out house had to do for the first few years of my life.

One of my earliest memories is when I was three or four years old. We were living in the garage while my father was building the house next door. I remember it had a dirt floor. There was a pot belly stove in the corner. It was a cold night with snow on the ground. We were very poor, as were all my cousins who lived in a row on the street. A few blocks south of Market Street, the Rock Island railroad ran along the Illinois River. In those days, they used steam engines. Near us was a water tank where they would stop the trains for water. My Dad and his friends would climb-up on the coal tender and throw coal to the ground while they stopped for water. The day I'm talking about was a day they stole coal from the train. Unbeknown to them, the railroad started soaking their coal in oil so it would burn hotter. My Dad put it in the old pot belly stove. The stove turned red hot and then white hot. My Mom ran next door and got a neighbor. My Dad knocked off the stovepipe chimney, and they slid two 2x4's under the stove, and they carried it outside to keep it from burning down the garage!

Another very memorable moment was on December 7, 1941, I was five years old. It was Sunday morning, my cousin from Pennsylvania George Schell was visiting us. He had just gotten out of Boot Camp at Fort Leonard Wood, Missouri, and was on leave. We were listening to the radio and suddenly President Roosevelt came on the air and we heard about the attack on Pearl Harbor. My cousin George solemnly said, well that's it, I'm probably going to die. Well, his prediction came true, he was killed in the battle to retake Italy in 1943.

Even at five years old, one of the things I was most impressed with was the United States ability to organize and mobilize for war. My town of Peru, Illinois had a city park called Washington Park. Within three months of December 7, 1941, the government had set up a recruiting and basic training camp in Washington Park with tents and soldiers marching in training and learning how to clean a rifle. I would go up and watch in awe and listen to their foul language of course. I wanted to memorialize things like this because many people don't know these minute details of the war. The U.S. went from a combined military force of around 250,000 to over 6,000,000 in less than a year.

In spite of his flaws, my Dad was an entrepreneur. By the time the war started, he already had four kids and was over 30 years old, so he didn't get drafted. Recognizing the fact that all automobile production was halted, he knew that replacement parts would be hard to come by, so he rented a 10 acre parcel of land from an older man named Walt Lewis right on busy Route 6 (replaced by interstate 80 today). He sold the brand new house he had just finished two years earlier that he built for the unheard of cost of $500 for a whopping $2,500. With this money he started a junk yard of wrecked cars. My Dad was right, he soon had a booming business. The going wage at that time was about $50 a week. In 1944, I remember him bragging that he was making over $500 a week. Meat was rationed at that time and so was gasoline and tires, so my job at eight years old was when a wrecked car came in, was to siphon the gasoline out of the car and check and see if the tires were good.

Soon, my Dad had bees, because sugar was also rationed. He fenced in the junkyard and we had pigs, chickens and rabbits. So rationing didn't effect us much.

My brother and I literally grew up with wrenches in our hands. When a customer came in needing a generator for a 1939 Chevy, my Dad would send my brother and me into the junkyard to take it off a wrecked car. My mechanical skills were developing a foundation.

In 1945, as the war was beginning to wind down, my Dad gave my brother and I two 1933 Plymouths. One, the rear end was wrecked, and the other, the front end was wrecked. He said if you can make a car out of them, I will let you sell it and keep the money. My twelve year old brother and I spent the summer making one good car out of two. We sold it to an Army Sergeant returning from the war in Europe for $75. We were rich!

My formal education started in kindergarten in 1941 at Roosevelt School. I think my most valuable lesson from kindergarten was on the first day. One spoiled girl was acting-up, and the teacher put her across her knee and spanked her! It was traumatic enough for me, so that I was a model student the rest of my life. I personally think the first grade is by far the most important year of your life. If you don't have a good teacher that teaches you to read, you are handicapped for life. I was fortunate my first grade teacher, Miss Burkenbuel was the best. She was 93 years old! She taught my Grandmother! My second grade teacher was excellent as well, Miss Burke and she was only 90! As I mentioned earlier, my Dad sold our house in Peru and we moved to Spring Valley, Illinois where I went to third grade. Peru schools were so much better than the Spring Valley schools that they thought both my brother and I should skip a grade. My Mom let my brother skip a grade, but thought that I was too small and immature and the older kids would pick on me. So, I stayed put in the third grade.

We only lived in Spring Valley for one year and we moved back to Peru. When I started the fourth grade, I was shocked to know my teacher was a Mrs. It was pretty much accepted in those days that teachers were all unmarried women. My, how times have changed!

As I mentioned, my Dad was making lots of money, but he didn't know how to keep it. I used to go to bars with him. It was legal in Illinois back then. He would say, "buy the house a round of drinks."

Things began to unravel soon after WWII ended. When they started making new cars, the used parts business waned. The man who rented the ten acres to my Dad offered to sell it to my Dad for $10,000. My Dad said, I'll give you $8,000. This man had been a good friend and mentor to my Dad. A week later, my Dad got a 30 day notice that he had sold the property to a third party for $12,000.

Unbeknownst to me, my Dad have been having an affair and my Mom and Dad got a divorce. We were now a family of six kids. Our whole world came crashing down. We moved back to Spring Valley to the seediest part of town into a house built in 1870 with an outhouse, well, and a pot belly stove for heat. So, we enjoyed the good life for the four war years. My Mom had to feed all seven of us on a whopping $30 a week child support!

I mentioned that I was small for my age and that I moved several times before the sixth grade. A new kid is not readily accepted at a new school unless you're a drop dead gorgeous girl or a really big guy yourself. The bullies of the school will pick on you. This is where I learned to be creative and think quick. I had this one big bully started picking on me in the fifth grade. I noticed a large group of boys about 50 feet away. I told him that he better leave me alone or I would call my big brother. He said where's your big brother? I said right over there and I pointed to the group of boys. He said, which one? I pointed to the biggest boy in the group. He grabbed my collar and said, I don't believe you! I yelled hey Dick help! He let go and ran away. My real brother Dick was already in High School!

In our trip down the road of life, I always like to look back to what I call the fork on the road where one makes a life altering decision that probably completely changes your life. Below was probably my first and the most profound.

In 1948, Hamilton Maze hired me to mow his lawn at his home. I was a dirt poor kid living in Spring Valley. My Mom and Dad were divorced. With my first paycheck from Mr. Maze, I bought the first new pair of shoes I ever owned. I was twelve years old. I worked for Mr. Maze for six years. Mr. Maze was probably the richest man in the county. He owned the Maze Lumber Company, the Maze Nail Factory and thirty or so other companies around the country. He had his own observatory on his lawn, dome and all. In the beginning, Mr. Maze would drive to Spring Valley every Saturday and pick me up, so I could mow his lawn. When I turned sixteen, he asked me what my plans were when I graduated from high school. When you're poor, your aspirations aren't very high. I told him that I would probably get a job at Wesclock Clock Factory. He said Wayne, I think you have more in you than that. I would like to take you to Chicago and have you take some aptitude tests at the Illinois Institute of Technology. I accepted, and he paid for me to stay at a hotel, and paid $300 for me to take the tests in 1953. When he got the results back, he told me I should go to college and become an engineer. I went on to LaSalle, Peru and Oglesby Junior College. I moved to California in 1959. I started my own manufacturing company in 1969. I went back to visit Mr. Maze in 1976 and thanked him for making me the success I became. When he died in 1979, his son George was sorting through Mr. Mazes belongings and found those aptitude tests and mailed them to me. Today, my financial success is definitely attributable to Mr. Maze. I truly owe my success to his foresight and generosity. Hamilton Maze was truly a great man.

CHAPTER 2

The job mowing Mr. Mazes lawn was one of many. I and many other kids detasseled corn every summer for one of the many seed corn companies in the area. I think they still do this today. They have what they call two bull rows of corn with a desired property and then they have six female rows of corn with another desired property, and when the tassels are almost ready to pollinate, they hire kids to pull the tassels on the six female rows. Then, the bull rows can cross pollinate the female. It's a frantic time as it must all be accomplished in about a three week period. For kids it was hot, hard work and we worked twelve hour days, seven days a week for 50 cents an hour. The first year I did it, we had to walk through the fields and I was so short, I had to bend the stalks over to reach the tassels. The second year, they had new detasseling machines that had platforms that you stood on at tassel level to pull the tassels. A big improvement. The third year, I did it I was 15 years old and had just gotten my drivers license, so I got the prestigious job driving the machine for a whopping 75 cents an hour.

When I was fourteen, I and several of my high school friends got a job setting pins at a bowling alley. The bowling alley was on the second floor above a tavern. There was a dumbwaiter connecting the bowling alley to the tavern. When the bowlers wanted a drink, they would place their order on a pad and cash in the dumbwaiter, and a few minutes later, up would come their drinks. Well, it didn't take us kids long to figure out that the bartenders couldn't see who was placing the drink orders. You guessed it, we spent a lot of the money on beer! I did learn a valuable life lesson at the bowling alley. I thought I was a pretty smart kid and used to think for hours how I could automate pin settings. I even made a statement to my friends, this is one job they will never automate! Guess what? They automated pin setting in the 60s. Life's lesson for me was if you can't figure how to solve a problem you're just not educated enough, and new tools are being added to the toolbox all the time which can make the unachievable achievable. So, if you have a problem in life that you were unable to solve, you should revisit that problem occasionally, and maybe it's now achievable with your new knowledge or tools.

When I was about thirteen, a friend of mine, Richard Yankowski, came to our house by the dump to show me his brand new Cushman motor scooter. He said, hop on the back and take a ride with me. It's Halloween and we can go to a corn field and pick some corn. It's fun on Halloween to throw corn kernels at people's windows. It sounds like hail and people don't know what's happening. So, we stopped at a cornfield on a country road. I was in the cornfield breaking off ears of corn and tossing them to Rich. He would shuck off the corn husks and put the ears into the little trunk on the back of the Cushman. A farmer drove up. We knew we shouldn't be there, so I crouched down in the field and Rich closed the trunk full of corn, and lifted up the seat where the engine was. The farmer asked Rich, if he was having trouble. Rich said, yes it won't start. The farmer said like Hell, you're stealing corn! There were corn husks all over the ground. The farmer was no dummy.

Did you ever stop here?—try it next time

HOTEL KASKASKIA, LaSALLE'S BEST HOTEL

93334·N

This is where I was a bellhop, Hotel Kaskaskia.

He figured out that there must be two of us and one was hiding in the field. He said to Rich you either get your buddy to come out, or I'm taking you to jail. I reluctantly stood-up and came out. The farmer said, this field doesn't belong to me, it belongs to my neighbor, Mr. Barnaby. You two drive your scooter to that farmyard up there and Mr. Barnaby can decide what to do with you. We did as he said, and when Mr. Barnaby came out his neighbor said, I caught these two young men stealing your corn. Mr. Barnaby had a long beard. He stroked his beard thoughtfully and said, since you boys like picking corn so much, do you see that farm wagon over there? Well when you pick that full of corn you can go home. Lesson learned. That was the first and last time we did that.

When I was fifteen, I went to work at Sheldon Croissants Gas Station in Spring Valley pumping gas for 50 cents an hour, every Saturday and Sunday from 1:30 p.m. until 9:30 p.m. In the summer,

I would mow Mr. Mazes lawn on Saturday mornings before going to work for Sheldon Croissant in the afternoon. Mr Maze also sold boats and Johnson outboard motors, so I got some experience fixing outboard motors. Elmer Wagner was the chief mechanic. He was my neighbor, and I was friends with his son Ron Wagner. I am still friends with Ron today who lives in Bradenton, Florida and is now 84 years old. Elmer was a wonderful man, and a very patient and good teacher from whom I learned a lot of good skills. I spent several Thanksgiving and Christmas days working at the gas station and my Mom would send me a plate of food, so I wouldn't miss out completely.

The summer of my sophomore year, when I turned sixteen, I did work at Wesclocks Factory. They had over 8,000 employees at that time and I was impressed with their efficiency.

My Junior year in high school was the year I outdid myself. I started the fall semester getting a job as a bellhop at Hotel Kaskaskia in LaSalle. My first day on the job, Eisenhower was running for President. They were having a young Republican convention for women at the hotel. They filled my arms up with about 30 long skinny boxes that had long stemmed roses in them and told me to take them up to room 301. My arms were so full I could barely see over them. When I got to room 301, I couldn't knock, so I kicked the door. I could hear a lot of talking and one voice said, come on in. I said, I can't open the door, my hands are full. Someone opened the door and I walked in unable to see because of my armload. Then, as I started to put the roses on the table, I realized all these women were in their bras and panties! I dropped the roses and ran!

I worked at the hotel for four months and my fondest memories were taking so many notable big band leaders to their rooms. Spring Valley had a roller rink called Les Buzz, owned by Les Honsheid and Buzz Verrucchi. They renovated it and changed the name to The LesBuzz Ballroom and started booking big name bands every Saturday night. It was a resounding success. They drew huge crowds all the way from Chicago, 100 miles away.

Since the Hotel Kaskaskia was the only nice hotel for miles around, all the bands stayed there. I remember taking: Tommy Dorsey, Jimmy Dorsey, Les Paul and most notable Louis Armstrong to their rooms! He gave me a five dollar

That's me in the checkered shirt on the porch. That house was built in the 1870s and would be condemned by today's standards.

tip when minimum wage was 50 cents an hour!

One of the dumbest decisions I ever made was when all my friends were working the night shift from four to midnight at the rubber factory in Ladd, Illinois, they talked me into quitting that cushy job as bellhop to take a job as a mold operator at the rubber company. They paid $2 an hour, and you worked 40 hours a week. I was getting 50 cents an hour and twenty hours as a bellhop. What I didn't take into account was the factory deducted income tax and union dues, and when you consider I was averaging well over $5 an hour as a bellhop with tips and no income tax or union dues, I was way better off as a bellhop!

Keep in mind, I worked the above jobs and I still would work Saturday morning for Mr. Maze and Saturday and Sunday afternoon at the Shell gas station! How I managed to make the honor roll and get straight A's in physics that year, I will never know!

My brother Dick was only three years older than me, but he was four years ahead in school because he skipped a grade. So, when I graduated from eighth grade in 1950, Dick graduated from high school. Soon after he graduated the Korean War started, and Dick joined the Air Force. That made me the man of the house at 13 years old. With four younger sisters, this put a lot of responsibility on my shoulders. My Mom was the Mom everyone should have. She left school after the eighth grade. She never drove a car, but she was a fantastic cook and I will admire her always for raising us the way she did by herself. Half of everything I earned went to my mother to help with the household finances.

The end of my Junior school year brought the end to my job at the rubber factory, as their business slowed down. All of us high school kids got laid off. The fact that my birthday was on July 16th was problematic when I was young.

The previous year when I worked for Wesclock, they required you to be sixteen to work there. So, I got the job the day after I turned sixteen and missed half the summer. The summer between junior and senior years, I heard that the Chicago, Burlington and Quincy Railroad was hiring, but you had to be seventeen. I didn't want to miss a half of summer of work again, so I copied my birth certificate and altered it to make me a year older. I got the job, along with many of my classmates, replacing rails and putting in ties. It was very hard, hot work. The big boss came by one day in a car that drove on the rails. I heard him talking to my boss and say, I didn't know you had any wetbacks working for you this year? That's what they called illegal aliens in those days referring to then getting into the U.S., by swimming across the Rio Grand. I knew he was referring to me, because I get very tan in the summer. I brazenly said, man I'm not a wetback, I got here the respected way. I climbed the fence. He said really? My boss said, he's just pulling your leg, he's just another one of these high school kids and was born here and isn't Mexican at all. A week later, they had a layoff and that big boss said you know that kid that stood-up to me? I like his moxie, I have a new job for him. I went from the hardest job I ever had, to the easiest job. I worked on a machine that drove on the tracks and loosened the gravel around the ties so water would drain away and not rot the ties. It moved about one mile an hour and my job was to pull a lever when we came to a road or obstruction, and a hydraulic ram would lift the blade and I would put it back down on the other side. I do remember that I had a 1940 Plymouth at the time and I had parked it under a tree that had thorns. My tires were so bald that when I got off work, all four of my tires were flat. There was no calling Triple AAA back in 1953, but you did carry a pump and a tire patch kit for just such occasions!

When the summer ended and I went back to

school for my senior year, I had mostly everything I needed to graduate, so the school let me get off at 1 p.m. and I got a job working for The Daily News Tribune in LaSalle, catching and bundling the newspapers for the paper routes. I worked from 1 to 4 .m. every week day. I mentioned my 1940 Plymouth. Well, when the weather turned cold, I started having trouble getting it started. The old six volt battery and poor condition was more than it could handle when the weather got cold. But, being resourceful, I found a hill about three blocks west of the newspaper that went down to the Illinois River. I would park the car on the hill with the front tires turned into the curb and go to work every day. When I got off work, I would jump in turn on the key and put it in second gear, turn the wheels away from the curb and coasted down the hill, I let out the clutch and the car would start and away I would go. It worked like a charm for several months and then one day I went to get it and it wasn't there. I thought wow, it must have rolled down the hill into the river. I thought, great it's such a piece of junk, maybe I can get the insurance and get a better car. I walked to the bottom of the hill and the guard rail wasn't broken so it must be stolen. I called the police to report it stolen. The police said, was it a blue 1940 Plymouth? I said yes. He said, it wasn't stolen, it was towed and its in the impound lot next to the police station. I walked to the police station and told the officer on duty I was there to pick up my 1940 Plymouth. He said that will be a $20 dollar fine and $30 for towing. I said my car isn't worth $50, besides, what did I do wrong? He said, that the mailman had been driving down that hill at 2 o'clock every day and that the car was abandoned because it's been there for months. I said, that's not true, I've been driving it every day and explained why I parked on the hill. The chief of police had been listening in on the conversation and walked over. He waived the fine and paid the towing charge out of his own pocket!

Because I worked so much during high school, I never participated in extracurricular activities. Plus, I didn't have much time for dating. I always loved school and never missed a day or was late in my life. We always had at least one period of study hall and I always worked hard and got all my homework done in study hall. I never took homework home. Thank goodness, because I wouldn't have had time for it anyway. I have been blessed that learning has always come easy.

I don't think I would have garnered the respect that I got, if it hadn't been for luck. I became good friends with the best looking and most popular guy in school, Dick Schweikert. The reason we became friends is where the luck comes in. In class, they always seated you alphabetically. Since my name was Schell and his was Schweikert, we sat next to each other in all our classes. Dick was a smart guy, but I had an edge on him and we used to do homework together. Dick was class President and Captain of our State champion undefeated football team, and knew of my problems at home and always made sure that I was included when the in crowd had an event. He went to good university on a football scholarships.

The summer after I graduated from high school I went back to work on the The Chicago, Burlington and Quincy Railroad. Sometimes your lies catch up to you. Remember when I lied about my age last year, telling them I was seventeen to get the job well now I was supposed to turn 18 in July. That meant you had to sign up for the draft and the railroad wanted proof. I stalled them off until time to start college and quit before they fired me.

College was much more demanding of my time than high school because there was so much more required homework, plus the fact that I was working multiple jobs, my grades were mediocre. I went to LaSalle, Peru and Oglesby Junior College which now called Illinois Valley Central College.

CHAPTER 3

The next crossroad on my road through life came in the summer of 1955. A friend of mine, Dan Andes, said to me, "Caterpillar in Peoria is hiring and I hear it's a good place to work, but I don't have a car. I will pay you Wayne if you will drive me to Peoria so I can apply?" Peoria was 60 miles away, so we jumped in my car and drove down. We found Caterpillars personnel office and I thought heck, while I'm waiting I might as well apply too because I'm kind of in limbo right now. An interviewer called me in and said, have you ever considered a tool and die apprenticeship? You go to school four hours a day and learn to run machines four hours a day. I said, I can't afford to go to school anymore, I need a paying job. He said, oh you get paid for eight hours a day only not quite as much as a factory worker. Eureka, I had found my calling. I couldn't believe my luck. I was made for this with my experience in my early years working in my Dads junkyard. The classes were all subjects very relevant to manufacturing. No meaningless required subjects like literature. I was in heaven. I loved the subjects and I went from a mediocre student in college to number one in my class. After six months of school, four hours a day and four hours of learning machines. Caterpillar put you out in the factory running actual production machines. This taught you the need for speed and efficiency. They didn't want you to get bored, so when your instructor felt you had mastered that particular machine, they would move you to a new one. Because of my mechanical background and love for what I was doing, I changed machines about twice as fast as was normal. I think one of the keys to anyone's success is to love what you're doing. Hardly a day has gone by since that fateful day when I started that tool and die apprenticeship where I can't wait to get to work. I wish everyone could be as lucky as I was in choosing a profession you truly love. Caterpillar's apprenticeship program was so good that many of its presidents started as apprentices.

Just to let you know that my young life wasn't work all the time I did take vacations.

Mine was with my much talked about 1950 Olds. I was a tool and die apprentice at Caterpillar in Peoria, Illinois, just before entering the Marines in 1956. The first two weeks in July, the factory shut down for vacation. Two apprentice buddies and I decided to vacation in Boulder, Colorado and drove there in my 1950 Olds. It was a great place for a vacation for three nineteen year old guys. Number one you only had to be 18 in Colorado to drink back then, plus Boulder is a college town with plenty of good looking girls.

We met some girls and decided to drive-up into the mountains with them. We ended up driving down this very rough gravel road. We hit a huge pothole and a rock punctured my gas tank. Gas began running out not too fast but I turned around and drove back to a small town we had just driven through. It had only one gas station with a mechanic, the owner. He said, I can't do a permanent fix on your tank and the only place you can get a new tank is in Boulder or Denver. But, I can do a temporary fix for you and won't even charge you. I said great. He said do you see that grocery store over there? I want you to buy a bar of Fels Naptha soap. Don't get any other kind, it has to be Fels Naptha. Sure enough they had Fels Naptha at the store. I think I paid about a quarter for it. I handed it to him. He took the bar of soap out of the package and it wasn't very hard you could kneed it like dough. He made a big ball with it and slapped it onto my gas tank over the leak and it stopped leaking immediately. He said that should get you back to Boulder. He said just don't drive it through any mud puddles. It's not affected by gasoline, but it was made to dissolve in water.

I actually ended up driving it all the way back home to Peoria with my Fels Naptha fix. My only insurance policy was I bought an extra bar of soap just in case of a rainstorm!

In October of 1956, I was about to be drafted, so I joined the Marines instead. This interrupted my apprenticeship. Another crossroad. When you join the military they usually determine your military occupational specialty when you join. They asked me what did you major in college? I told them mechanical engineering. They said the Marines don't need mechanical engineers. They said any other skills? I said I'm in a tool and die apprenticeship at Caterpillar. The recruiter said the Marines don't need any toolmakers. He then asked do you have any hobbies? I said I like hot rod cars. The recruiter said great you're a mechanic. The Marines need mechanics!

CHAPTER 4

My years in the Marines had many critical forks in the road. One of the reasons I joined the Marines was that they had a very attractive program called NAVCAD. Short for Naval Aviation Cadets. If you qualified after boot camp, you would be sent to Pensacola, Florida, and enter the NAVCAD program and after two years of training you would come out an officer and either a helicopter pilot or jet fighter pilot. Before being accepted there were many hurdles to jump. It started with a preflight physical and the requirement that you have a bachelors degree or pass a rigorous college equivalency test. Since I only went to junior college, I had to take the college equivalency test. I did and passed. There were three other recruits trying out for the program with me. Two of the three passed all the tests and when boot camp was completed, they went directly to Pensacola into NAVCAD. I had to send back to Illinois for my high school and college records. My LPO college records didn't show up in time, and I couldn't leave directly from boot camp. I found out later that LPO was in the process of shutting down and morphing into Illinois Valley Junior College which was under construction.

After three months of boot camp, and six weeks of infantry training at Camp Pendleton, I got a 30-day leave. After leave, I was assigned to Twentynine Palms Marine base with an MOS for auto mechanic. I wasn't looking forward to becoming an auto mechanic. But, upon arriving at my new assigned 155 gun battalion, I was presented another fork on the road.

I was always a pretty squared away Marine. I showed up in pressed and starched dungarees and shined boots and a fresh Marine haircut. The other new recruits checking in with me all looked like they were just coming off a 30 day leave, all disheveled. The Captain checking me in, looked me up and down and said, Private Schell, I need a driver for Colonel Crottinger the Battalions Commanding Officer. How bad do you want to be an auto mechanic? The Colonels driver doesn't have to stand guard duty or mess duty. So with luck and being squared away, I became the driver for the C.O.

My college transcripts finally showed-up a few months later and they proceeded with my processing for NAVCAD. I was sent to El Toro Marine Base and took a very vigorous flight physical. I passed and the final hurdle was an interview in front of a board of officers. The head of the board was my commanding officer Colonel Crottinger. He had taken an immediate liking to me as his driver, and I passed the board and my application went on to Pensacola, Florida and I waited for reassignment. Months went by, and meanwhile, I had met my first wife and we got married on December 7, 1957. I immediately notified my superior so that I could get the perks of being married. On December 11, my orders arrived announcing I was accepted to NAVCAD. I was devastated at the time because after waiting nine months, I didn't think they would accept me. What was devastating was if you were married you were no longer eligible. This was a very major change in direction on the road of life.

At 20 years old with my 1950 Olds while in the Marines.

Think about it, I'm six weeks older than John McCain. Had I gone into NAVCAD in 1957 after the first year, I would have been required to reenlisted for six more years, that would have had me getting out in 1964. By that time, the Vietnam War was escalating. I would have probably ended up as a pilot in Vietnam suffering the same fate as John McCain, or worse.

One weekend, a bunch of Generals from the Pentagon came to the base and my C.O. asked me if I would take them out on the range for a tour, and they wanted to go rock hunting. He said, I told them you probably knew your way around the base better than anyone. That was an interesting weekend for sure. We didn't get back to the main base until late Sunday afternoon. I usually got to keep the Colonels prized Jeep inside the motor pool. Getting back so late, it was already closed. So, I was forced to park it on the line outside with the peon Jeeps.

When I returned on Monday morning, I was shocked to find someone had taken a knife and for a lack of a better word, keyed the hood badly. I was sick. It wouldn't polish out and the knife cut so deep, it would still show even if I repainted it. Never daunted, I came up with a brilliant solution. There were several Jeeps sitting on the line with major repairs required waiting to be taken to the main repair facilities to be fixed; with the permission of the motor transport sergeant, I removed the hood of one of those Jeeps with the plan to make it well painted and shiny and when it was ready, I would switch hoods and put the scratched hood on the Jeep waiting to be taken in for repairs. That way the C.O.s Jeep would always have a hood through out the process.

Like every well laid plan, things go wrong. The day before I was ready to switch hoods, the broken down Jeeps got towed away. The motor transport sergeant says, Schell they're looking everywhere for that hood and we have a General's inspection tomorrow. You have to get rid of the hood! Twentynine Palms is in the middle of the desert. How do you get rid of a Jeep hood? I waited till everyone was at the mess hall and walked out into the sand parking area with a shovel and dug a hole and buried the scratched hood. As far as I know it's still there.

Meanwhile, life went on as the Colonels driver, but to be honest, it wasn't a very fulfilling job for me. I wasn't creating anything and had very little responsibility and just sat around a lot in case the Colonel wanted to go somewhere. Meanwhile, the Captain in charge of the maintenance of the 155 mm self propelled guns knew my MOS was auto mechanic, plus he had access to my personal files and remarked more

than once that he knew I got a higher score on my IQ test than anyone in the Battalion except the Colonel. He thought I was wasting my time and talent driving. I never had to stand guard duty, but I was required to stand by in the Battalion office once a month to answer the phones on weekends. This particular weekend, the maintenance Captain Wade happened to be officer of the day while I was on phone watch. He started his sales pitch to get me to come to work for him as a mechanic. He said, just think about it, you would have a good career when you got out of the Marines. I said, I already have a good career started. I'm half way through a tool and die apprenticeship at Caterpillar. He said, do you mean you know how to run a machine shop? Being me, I had to brag and said of course.

On Monday morning, my C.O. Called me into his office and Captain Wade was with him. Captain Wade said, Colonel, did you know that Schell knows how to run a machine shop? The Colonel says, no is that true Private Schell? I said, yes Sir. He proceeded to tell me the story about a five ton truck sitting next to the maintenance building that had a fully equipped machine shop on the back of it. It seems a year before the Force Artillery Group, the arm of maintenance that does all major repairs, sent two Marines in this five ton mobile machine shop over to do repair work on our 155 guns. There was a flair-up in Lebanon and the two marines who brought the machine shop to the 155 gun battalion were transferred overnight to Lebanon. A few weeks went by and no one from Force Artillery Group showed up to retrieve the machine shop. So Captain Wade moved it into the shop and repainted it as a vehicle of the 155 gun battalion. Yes, he stole it! Now, the 155 has a full machine shop with no one who knows how to run it. The Colonel says, Schell, I can't make you since it's not your MOS, but half of my guns are out of commission because I can't get parts. Would you step up? I'm sensing maybe I have a

March 1957 Camp Pendleton, California.

little bargaining leverage here. I say, "Sir I don't have to stand guard duty driving you." He immediately responded, "you won't have to stand guard duty." I said, "Sir, I have a darn good chance of being promoted to corporal in a few months driving you." He said, "if you do me a good job you'll be corporal in a few months."

I took over the machine shop and of course, I loved doing it. I was making parts and actually making a difference. I no longer felt guilty getting a paycheck, and oh yes, within a month I had all those guns up and running and six weeks later, I got promoted.

After I had done all the military repairs, the word got out that I could make things. Soon, I was grinding valves for officers cars and making other things. I even made some fancy brass shifting knobs for the Colonels' Jeep. I was still single at this time, and one day a lieutenant stopped by and told me about a hotel in town run by two older sisters called El Adobe Hotel, and they were looking for a handyman if I needed extra income. I went and talked to them. I hated living in the barracks, so I offered that if they would give me a hotel room in exchange for me taking care of their pool and any other work, and they would pay me a dollar an hour. I went to work for them and now I was living at a resort where on weekends the pretty girls would come to me, and I no longer had to tolerate barracks life. Life in the Marines isn't that bad if you're creative!

I've been one who either likes to pull a joke or tell a joke. While out in the desert on maneuvers at 29 Palms as the commanding officer's driver, I was called into the command tent. There were three generals and four or five colonels including my C.O.

When training, they try to replicate real war conditions as closely as possible. Since

Twentynine Palms is a artillery base, the battalions are various types on big guns and rockets. They are typically spaced miles apart firing on common targets miles down range. When I walked into the tent, I was handed a dispatch case and one General said, Pfc Schell, Colonel Crottinger told me that you know the base better than anyone else. We need you to hand deliver these messages to each battalion commander and since we are operating under war conditions, you can't turn on your headlights. You have to use the blackout lights your Jeep is equipped with. So off I went with minimal lights. I dutifully delivered the messages to each battalion.

On my way back, a little baby skunk ran across my path. When I was a boy, my Uncle had a pet skunk that he caught as a baby and had it de-scented. I learned from him that skunks don't get their scent until they are almost full grown. Knowing this, I jumped out of the Jeep and caught the baby skunk. I wrapped it up in my field jacket and took it with me. I walked into the command tent with all the Colonels and Generals and announced: Look at the baby kitten I found out in the desert. I opened up my field jacket and when they saw the baby skunk they almost tore the tent down getting out. Later Colonel Crottinger said to me, Schell if it wasn't so damn funny, I would have court marshalled you.

Life changed on December 7, 1957, I got married. I moved into base housing; an 8 foot wide 32 foot long mobile home. My daughter Cindy was born while I was in the Marines on September 18, 1958. I pretty much served the rest of my time in the Marines uneventfully. When I got out, I drove back to Illinois with my new family to move on with my life and finish my tool and die apprenticeship.

CHAPTER 5

Upon returning to Illinois my plan for immediately returning to Caterpillar and finishing my apprenticeship hit a bump in the road. They were on strike! As good of a company as they were, you could expect two or three shutdowns a year for strikes, or the steel mills would go on strike and Caterpillar would shut down for lack of steel. Back in those days, all of Caterpillars production was in one location, East Peoria, Illinois. They had over 30,000 employees. Peoria lived and died with Caterpillars fortunes. They have since learned and have plants located throughout the world, thus, if one plant went on strike they weren't hurt so badly.

Meanwhile, I had a family to feed and couldn't afford to sit around and wait. While I was in the Marines, my mother and father got back together and remarried. They were still on the same property in Spring Valley, but my Dad had built a new home. I purchased a new 8x36 foot mobile home for $3,000 and parked it on their property. My Uncle had a business sharpening farm discs. He was busy and needed a helper. He had this disc sharpening machine mounted on the back of a pickup truck and would go to the farm. You had to dismantle the disc and sharpen the blades one at a time, and then reassemble the disc. It was hard work, but the pay was good. Finally, Caterpillar called me back. I commuted 60 miles each way for three months and then moved my mobile home to Peoria.

I was now making a whopping $1.75 an hour. I now had a son and daughter, so it was tight for a family of four to live. That's when my lifelong ambitions kicked in. Knowing how lucrative the disc sharpening business was, and since I now was a skilled disc sharpener, I drove to Washington, Iowa in my newly acquired 1946 Studebaker truck that I bought for $300. I talked the man who was making the sharpening machines into selling me one for $1,200 putting $300 down and a year to pay the balance. So, for $600 I was in the disc sharpening business (MY OWN BUSINESS) Wow! I was an instant success and I would work at Caterpillar on the graveyard shift, come home and have breakfast and sharpen farm discs during the day. Come home and have dinner and sleep until about 10 p.m. and back to Caterpillar. I could make more in one day sharpening farm discs than I made in a week at Caterpillar. The only problem it was seasonal: in the spring, when the farmers were getting ready to use them, and in the fall when they were ready to put them away for the winter. But, hey we had food on the table.

Caterpillar went on another strike and it was winter time so there was no work for my disc sharpening business, but I had heard that Sitterlies Sand and Gravel in my hometown had a big government contract, so I got a job there picking mud balls out of gravel.

They were very busy with a government contract working 24-7. I worked seven days a week, 12 hours a day. Hard work, but good money at the time. The interstate highway system built a test road between LaSalle and Ottawa of all different types of road base and concrete. When it was completed, they ran trucks over it 24-7 for evaluation. Why did they pick the Illinois valley? The engineers had determined that the Illinois valley has the most severe road conditions in the nation because more freezing and thawing occurs there than anywhere else in the country. And now you know the rest of the story!

Finally, Caterpillar went back to work, so I took a big cut in pay and went back to my apprenticeship. Shortly after I completed my apprenticeship, Caterpillar went out again and this time I thought it was going to be a long one, so I moved my mobile back to my parents yard, and we went to California to visit my wife's parents. I got what I thought would be a temporary job as a leadman at a company called the Deutsch Company supervising about 30 women on an aircraft electric connector assembly line. It was winter in Illinois and the weather was beautiful in California, so we decided to give up on Caterpillar and remain in California. I went back briefly to sell my disc sharpening business, my mobile home and arranged for a moving company to bring the rest of our belongings to California. I've never regretted the decision.

CHAPTER 6

Deutsch Company in Banning was the worst company I ever worked for in my long career. I was a toolmaker which they didn't need, but they needed a leadman to supervise about 30 women who assembled electrical connectors used in aerospace. I replaced a man whom they had fired. They promised me a big raise within six months. We got an apartment for $60 a month. I was making $2.25 an hour. My father-in-law Pete was a good guy, but he was an alcoholic. He was dealt some bad cards in his life, probably had a lot to do with his drinking. He bought a very busy Richfield gas station. Today, they're called ARCO. It was right on the main highway going from Los Angeles to Palm Springs in 1953. His was the very first business entering Banning. On the weekends, the traffic was bumper-to-bumper, so his business was booming. Two years after he bought it, they built the 10 freeway, totally bypassing Banning. Overnight, his business dropped by about two thirds. He was an excellent mechanic, although he had pints of whiskey hidden all over the shop. He was right on the edge of the Morongo Indian reservation. He did a lot of business on credit. He complained he was so busy that he could never take a day off, yet he never had any money. I started working for him and discovered that he had dozens of customers who weren't paying.

Here, I was a 25 year old young man and I started telling my father-in-law how to run his business. I talked him into becoming a cash only business for a six months trial. Pete was right he wasn't nearly as busy, but he had more money in his pocket than he had in years. He finally could take a weekend off.

Back at Deutsch, they fired the foreman at a small factory in Beaumont and asked me to move there and take that job. No raise that would come later. By the way, the guy who replaced me got fired after two weeks. So now I put my six months in and still no raise as promised. Right before Memorial Day weekend, 1961, I gave them a two week notice. The next day, they fired me so they wouldn't have to give me one day of holiday pay. So, I now took another another fork on the road of life.

CHAPTER 7

With Memorial Day weekend over and jobless, I had to find work. My Moms uncle was a fire chief for the City of Los Angeles, and had offered to open some doors to get on as a Fireman in Los Angeles. A fireman's job wasn't nearly as coveted back then as it is today. All their great perks have greatly expanded over the years. He arranged for me to get an interview.

I got in my car and was driving to LA for the interview driving on the 5 freeway in the City of Commerce, and I saw a sign on a factory next to the freeway "Machinists Wanted." I got off the freeway and went in to apply for the job. The opening was on the afternoon shift for a lathe operator. The interviewer looked over my application. I have horrible hand writing. He said, I see you've been making $2.75 an hour. The best I can offer you is $2.85 an hour, He thought my two was a seven, my lousy handwriting got me fifty more cents an hour. I said, I will take it. Another very life changing path on the road of life.

My family and I moved to an apartment in Commerce in May 1960. The company I went to work for was Kaynar manufacturing. They had two main products. One, you may have heard of called Lady Ellen Hair Clips "Clippies." Women's hair styles in the 60s had a lot of curls. Kaynar was making hundreds of thousands of them every day. The other product was aircraft fasteners, nuts and bolts. I was working in the fastener division.

I put my three months in, and as promised, they gave me a performance review, and told me they were giving me ten cents an hour raise. I had noticed that they were advertising for a toolmaker on the sign outside that initially brought me in. I said, instead of the raise how about giving me a chance to show you what I can do in that toolmaker job that's open. I got the toolmaker job and the raise. The department I worked in made the tooling for drilling and tapping department. I got the job in August, and in September they announced that the two partners were splitting-up and Frank Klause was going to be the sole owner of the fastener division, and that he was building a new factory in Fullerton, California and we would be moving in eight months to Fullerton. In October, they announced that they were starting a third shift to build-up inventories for the move shutdown.

They announced that the foreman of the Tapping Department was being promoted to plant manager of the third shift, and they were looking for someone with management experience to take charge of the Tapping Department for the build-up. I stepped forward and said, I can do it. That crummy job as leadman at Deutsch wasn't a total waste after all. They gave me the job as temporary foreman and I went on salary with a raise. It was like putting a duck in water. I absolutely loved the challenge. Kaynar was everything Deutsch wasn't. They demanded excellence, but recognized exceptionalism and rewarded it.

When I took over the department, it had the worst rejection rate in the factory. I concentrated on this negative and instituted new procedures and checks and balances and in three months the Tapping Department went from the worst rejection rate, to the best. My temporary job became permanent. With my new found wealth, my family purchased our first home in Fullerton in December of 1961 for $15,500 with $500 down. The factory moved to Fullerton in the Spring of 1962. It grew from about 300 employees to over 1,000 by 1969.

I was promoted to general foreman in 1964 with over 300 employees reporting to me from five departments. In 1965, the company sent me to England for four months to set-up a new factory in Wembley to sell fasteners to a new company, Airbus.

An interesting story that is kind of appropriate here. I'm now 83 and not old enough to be in WWII, but I'm old enough to remember it. I lived just North of Hyde Park for four months. I became friends with a French Canadian who was about twelve years older than me and he was in WWII. He was in the RCAF and was stationed in Bournemouth during the war. After the war, he stayed and lived in Ireland. He was a booking agent for Irish show bands. One weekend, he said to me, I have to go down to Bournemouth to do some business, would you like to go along? I did and that's when he told me about being stationed there during the war. We checked into the hotel in Bournemouth. It was cold, rainy and the city was pretty quiet. We asked the clerk where there was a good place to eat and maybe some lively entertainment. He recommended a casino down a country road in the New Forest. We thought we were lost, and suddenly, there were cars parked everywhere. We had found the casino. In those days in England, you had to be a member to get into casinos. They had an exception for Americans (Americans had money), we got in. The place was huge, there were hundreds of people and several bars. We stopped at this one bar and ordered a drink. While we waited for the woman bartender to get our drinks, he said, I'm almost positive I dated the bartender during the war. I said no way! When she returned with the drinks he identified himself, and sure enough they had dated during the war. He started asking about some of his English friends he had met while stationed there. She said, well your old friend Hank is one of owners of the Casino and he's sitting at the other bar over there. We went to the other bar and sure enough there was Hank. I'll never forget the meeting of these two war buddies and needless to say, I never had to buy another drink all night. This is only one of many reasons I have such a soft spot for Brits!

In 1967, I became president of the Kaynar management club and had never met Frank Klause the owner, but I came up with factory tours and a behind the scenes tour of Knotts Berry Farm, with Walter Knott himself as our tour guide. Attendance swelled from thirty or forty, to over two hundred including Frank Klause himself. We actually became good friends and he would come out in the factory and ask my advice. In 1968, things changed dramatically. Frank Klause sold Kaynar to a large corporation for $36,000,000. We no longer had the close knit family and we had to submit requests to corporate to purchase new equipment. I was heading to a new fork in the road of life.

CHAPTER 8

As the confines of corporate management got worse, I grew more and more disenchanted with my dream job. Plus, corporate management put a higher value on education and a degree than on actual accomplishments. This I believe holds true today, and I think is one of the main causes for the demise of major corporations such as General Motors and General Electric. I could no longer see an opportunity for advancement based on performance. A competitor from New Jersey had heard of my achievements through a former engineer who had worked for Kaynar, and now worked for them. They flew me back to New Jersey and offered me the job as their plant manager at twice the pay I was currently making. After touring the not so great city of Union, New Jersey, I decided that it was not worth leaving beautiful Southern California even for twice the money.

One of the best machines on the market for drilling and tapping nuts was made by Snow Manufacturing from Bellwood, Illinois. Over the years, I had purchased over 40 of them for Kaynar. I loved innovating them. I made them perform far better than the manufacturer was able to. The west coast representative was a guy named Frank Zila. His father had owned a large manufacturing company called Zila Manufacturing. His dad sold the business in 1965 for $6 million dollars in cash and retired. He died in 1967, and left $300,000 to each of his two sons. In those days, that was a small fortune. So Frank wasn't too hard pressed to sell machines. He new that I was unhappy at Kaynar and knew that I probably knew the business better than

anyone. He offered me a job selling Snow Tapping machines at the same salary that I was making, plus a company car and expenses. At this point in my life, I didn't have a very high opinion of salesman. But, my brother Dick had been a very successful salesman, so I called him as I had done many times in life for advice. He first asked me, are the machines a good product? I said well, I've bought more than 40 of them for Kaynar. Then he asked, are you knowledgeable about them? I said probably the most knowledgeable of anyone on the planet! The final question he asked was, can the machines make or save your customers money? I said without a doubt! He said, well, then your problem won't be getting in to see your customers, it will be getting out the door. When they find out that you really know what your doing, they will want to pick your brain for knowledge.

I gave notice at Kaynar. Kaynar had no idea how involved I was in all aspects of manufacturing over and above my own departments. I really cared. My final big achievement was that I was on the material review board. It consisted of the head of quality control, an engineer and me. We would get together once a week and evaluate batches of rejected nuts to make a decision whether to scrap, sort or in some way correct the defect.

We were looking at a batch of 100,000 Boeing engine nuts that had failed to achieve the required removal torque from Kaynar's patented self locking feature. They were very much needed by Boeing and they were worth over $100,000 to Kaynar. The other two members of the board wanted to scrap them but I had an idea how to correct the defect and they agreed to let me try my idea. This was a few weeks before I quit. My idea worked, they were accepted and shipped on my last day at Kaynar. I presented the results, pointed out the savings to my boss, the plant manager and said this is my going away present to Kaynar. He offered me a $25 a week raise to stay, and I declined. Apparently, they missed me even more than I thought they would, because six months after I left, they called me back to a board of directors meeting and offered to double my salary to return. But I had moved on with my life, and declined.

On to my new job selling. My first week on the new job (January 1969), there was a machine tool show in Los Angeles where my new boss Frank Zila had a booth with Snow tapping machines on display. One day, this scruffy looking man stopped by the booth. He was chewing on an unlit stub of a cigar and he had a rope on for a belt! I have never judged anyone by there appearance, so I politely spent about half an hour answering his questions.

When he left, Frank asked me if I knew who that was? I said no. He said that was Ed Iskenderian of the legendary Iskenerian racing cam fame. Who knew! A few weeks later, I received a call from Ed and asked me to come to his factory in Gardena, California. I left with an order for four machines! I was off and running!

There were dozens of aerospace manufacturers in the Los Angeles basin back then. During my nine years at Kaynar, literally hundreds of foremen and engineers had come and gone. I don't know if you've ever experienced this, but I did. When a new employee comes on board, the older employees become defensive of their jobs, and are reluctant to help a new employee, and point out every obvious mistake the new employee is making. I think it's called job preservation.

Well, I was always super confident in my abilities and never worried about someone better than me getting my job. Therefore, all these new supervisors and engineers that passed through Kaynar were people that I would go out of my way to be helpful to, never realizing how much it would help me in my new sales job.

All of these past Kaynar employees were now scattered throughout the aerospace industry. Once I realized this, the first thing I would do when I called on a new factory, I would ask to see the factory phone directory, and sure enough there was someone I knew so that I could get a foot in the door. Boy, did it work! As soon as we reconnected, without exception, I was introduced to other key employees as the person that knew more about tapping than anyone. At the end of my first year, because my sales were through the roof, I had been promised a big bonus. My boss Frank whom had quickly blown through that $300,000 inheritance from high living, didn't have the money for my bonus. I said well, give 10% of the stock in the company. He did just that. Now, I was a partner!

The next year, 1970 was even better. I contacted the company that I used to buy most af my taps from Sossner Tap, to see if my new partner and I could get a distributorship. They immediately agreed. Now, instead of a one time sale of a machine, we were selling the perishable tools that the machine used and had to be purchased over and over.

Next, I called on many smaller machine shops that had drilling and tapping, but not enough to justify buying their own machine. They would say honestly, tapping is one of our biggest problems. Do you know someone who specializes in tapping so we can outsource it? Tapping really is a science in itself. Many elements go into successfully tapping, especially in large volume or on exotic metals. I looked into tapping services and they were virtually nonexistent.

So, I told my partner we should start a company called Specialty Tapping Company. We did, initially using the three new Snow Tapping machines that we had as demos. We bought a mill, lathe and grinder to make the required tooling. I was initially the only employee making the tools, doing the drilling and tapping. I was right again, I recognized a need and filled the need. I still preach this to my nieces and nephews. If you want to be successful in a new business, first recognize the need and fill it. Uber is one of the newer examples of this.

We soon out grew our 400 square foot shop and leased a 4,600 square foot building on Alondra Boulevard in Gardena, (two blocks from Ed Iskenderia). By 1973, we had grown to 12 employees in Specialty Tapping. The supply company and offices were upstairs in about 600 square feet. The manufacturing took place on ground level about 4,000 square feet. Prior to us leasing it, it had been occupied by a company making rain lamps during that craze.

In 1973, things started to change. Frank who had always been a good honorable guy and good friend changed dramatically when his mother died. His Mom left Frank's rogue brother $10,000 and willed Frank $4,000,000. Frank immediately started spending like the money was in his account. He bought a beautiful home behind the gates in Palos Verdes on four acres, he bought a condo in Mammoth and a big motor home. Then his troubles began. His brother contested the will and as things like this always do, it drug on for years. Meanwhile, he started taking more than his share of the money from our two businesses. Meanwhile, I had always remained good friends with my old boss Frank Clause. I went to auctions for him and got him good deals on machinery. I went to factories he owned around the world as a consultant, and even worked out with him at the gym.

I mentioned to him one day about my partners

lavish lifestyle and the way he was going he was going to bankrupt us. He said, why don't you buy him out? I said I don't have any money. He said you negotiate and let me worry about how you will pay for it.

I negotiated the buyout with my partner Frank Zila agreeing to exchange my stock in the supply company plus $40,000 cash for Specialty Tapping, and I would own S.T. 100% and he would again own the supply company 100%. We agreed to share the building since we had one more year on the lease and when the lease expired, I would renegotiate the lease and he would either sublease or move when the lease expires.

I showed the agreement to Frank Klause and he set-up an appointment with his attorney. His attorney looked over my financials and said, I sure wouldn't do this loan, your net worth is 0. But, Frank says he has confidence in you and told me to do it. How long do you need to pay him back? I said think I can do it in ten years. I actually paid him back in three years. We did the buyout and after working six months of 14 hours a day, 7 days a week, I was just starting to get ahead and a new dilemma struck. The Friday before the Forth of July 1974, I got a letter from the IRS stating you owe $25,000 in back payroll taxes from 1973! My former partner had used the money instead of paying the taxes with the money. The IRS said if the didn't receive the entire amount by July 6 they would seize the assets and shut down my business. That was a pretty dark fourth. About three months prior to this, I had quoted a company in Irvine $100,000 to build four semiautomatic machines at $25,000 each. These machines would drill the stem holes in digital watch cases. They were on the ground floor of the burgeoning new digital watch industry. In my quote, I stated that I would require a 25% deposit with the order. When I returned to work on July fifth, sadly, thinking this would be the last day of Specialty Tapping's existence. As I

These are the watch cases that I built the four drilling machines for Casetel Corporation that saved my business.

opened my weekend mail here was a purchase order from Casetel for four drilling machines for $100,000, plus, a cashiers check for $25,000 as a down payment. I was saved. God surely works in mysterious ways. Granted, I still worked many long hours to fulfill the order for four machines.

When the lease expired on the building at the end of 1974, I started negotiating with the landlord for a new five year lease. We agreed on $800 a month. After a few weeks when I didn't receive it, I called the landlord to find out why. He said your partner stopped by last week and signed it. A few hours later my former partner Frank stopped by and said with a smirk, I decided to get the new lease and on March first your new rent would be $800 per month. He was going to make me pay 100% of the rent and he would be upstairs rent free.

Well, Frank didn't know it, but my business was flourishing without his extravagance. I needed more space. I quietly started looking for a new home. I was now divorced from my first wife and living in a townhouse in Tustin. I needed a central location near a freeway. Cerritos was my most desired location. About six months before, I had seen this brand new 10,000 square foot industrial building was for sale. I had drooled over it, but it was way beyond what I could afford. Then, I went back a week later

and it had a sold sign on it. So now, six months later, I decided to look in Cerritos again and I couldn't believe my eyes the building I had coveted so much at the corner of 166th and Norwalk Blvd had a for sale or lease sign on it. I immediately called the realtor and offered to lease it, with a six month option to buy with all my rent going towards the down payment. He said, well it belongs to Dunn Properties in Irvine and your asking for a lot, but it has fallen out of escrow twice. I will see what I can do. He called me on a Friday morning and said, I have set-up an appointment for us this afternoon and you won't have to wait for an answer because we are meeting Mr. Dunn himself. When we walked into Mr. Dunn's office, I was greeted with: Wayne I didn't know it was you. I cannot believe my good luck Mr. Dunn was a friend of mine at the gym I went to in Tustin. I had no idea he was a big shot. Needless to say, he accepted my offer. Again God works in mysterious ways! For the next two months I worked feverishly preparing the new building for the move. The lease was up on the old building on March first and my former partner Frank left for a two week vacation on Thursday, February 25th, so on Friday morning my employees and I started moving. By Monday morning, Specialty Tapping was up-and-running at the new building in Cerritos, and Frank Zila was stuck with a five year lease on an empty building. I say don't get mad get even!

CHAPTER 9

One day during the transition from the old building in Gardena to the new building in Cerritos, I had to go to Cerritos to meet with an electrician. I told my foreman I might as well take that drilling machine with me since we won't need it again until after we move. So, he loaded it onto my little Toyota pick-up truck. I had bought a second fork lift anticipating the need for one at each location for loading and unloading. I estimated that it weighed about 1,000 pounds. I later found out if weighed almost 3,000 pounds. But, it was only twelve miles east on the 91 freeway. I pulled off on the Norwalk Blvd. off ramp. Only a block to go! A month or so earlier, they had dug a trench down Norwalk Blvd. for a new sewer line. When they covered it up and repaved over it they didn't do a very good job and it had a big dip in it. As I was sitting at the off ramp waiting for the light to turn green, I remembered this and thought I better be careful with all this weight. Meanwhile, while I'm waiting a CHP pulls up alongside me on the right. He's waiting to cross over and get back on the freeway at the on ramp on the other side. He looks at that big machine on that little Toyota and then looks down at my half flat tires. The lights turned green. I proceed across Norwalk Blvd. with the CHP turning left in the lane next to me. I hit the dip and the truck and machine begin to rock precariously. I slam on my brakes. The top heavy machine flips out of the truck bed just missing hitting the CHP car. I jump out of the truck and quickly apologizing to the CHP and I said, I have a forklift in that building pointing at Specialty Tappings new home would you please turn your lights on so no one will hit it until I can move it. He said you're damn right, I will because I plan on writing you a ticket when you're finished. I loaded it up and the CHP followed me to the factory with lights flashing. When I turned into the driveway, I heard him say on his bullhorn. It looks like you have enough problems and drove off.

With the move completed and plenty of room to expand, I was off and running. I secured a contract with my old employer Kaynar and started tapping the very parts that I used to do when I was an employee. My former partner Frank Zila's supply company didn't fair as well. We did have a non-compete clause in our partnership split-up, which lapsed after five years. I then started my own supply company called SF Supply. Sossner Tap and Tool had been bought out by a Japanese company called OSG Corporation. They were the largest tool manufacturing company in the world. They awarded me a distributorship, and within five years, I became their top sales distributor in the world. In 1988, they had a sales promotion where they offered one free week vacation at a resort in Barbados for every $50,000 increase in sales. By the end of the year, I had a $300,000 increase. That means I was awarded six free trips. By this time, I was remarried to my current wife, Suzanne. So we went along with my daughter, my wife's parents and her youngest sister. OSG ended up taking over four hundred people. I was the talk of the group because I was by far, the biggest increase. One Japanese distributor asked me how many sales people do you have to accomplish this? I said you're looking at him! Which was true. From 1975 to 1990, I was successful beyond my wildest dreams. Life was good.

Yes, it's Dolly Parton having lunch with me and my new bride back in 1984.

Dolly Parton

I came home from work one night in 1984 and my new bride of less than a year Suzanne was reading about a benefit radio auction for the City of Hope. She said, wow they're auctioning off cruises, trips to Hawaii and all sorts of things.She said it's for a really good cause and you can afford it, you should bid on something. Me being a smart ass said, maybe if they were auctioning a date with Dolly Parton I would do it. She said I think there is, and then says yes there is and it's coming up at 5 p.m., in twenty minutes. So, I called in and gave them all my information just in case I won. Most things were going for between $500 and $1,000. All the

other bidders dropped out when it went over $2,000 except one other person. The bidding for the date with Dolly got up to $3,200. I finally said, let the other person have it and hung up. About fifteen minutes later, the phone rang and it was the City of Hope saying Dolly was so thrilled that she could raise that much money that if I would match the $3,200 she would do it for both of us.

I had several choices for my date. She had just finished shooting the movie Rhinestone with Sylvester Stallone, and one of my options was to go to Fox Movie Studio's and watch Dolly and the Mike Post Orchestra put the music to the movie. They let me bring Suzanne along.

We watched and listened to the music for about two hours. Then we went to the Fox restaurant where they had a table with a sign "Rreserved for Dolly Parton." Mike Post joined us. While we were sitting there, many other noteable actors came by to say hello. During the course of conversation, someone mentioned it was April 17th. I said oh my gosh, I completely forgot today is my brothers birthday. I had a suitcase size cell phone in those days and said, would you please excuse me while I call Dick and wish him happy birthday? Dolly said would you like me to sing happy birthday to him? I called my brother and said happy birthday Dick. I have someone with me who wants to sing happy birthday to you. He said who? I said you figure it out. Dolly sang happy birthday to him and handed the phone back to me. Dick said she sounded just like Dolly Parton. I said it was. He said you better send me lots of pictures because no one will ever believe me. I can tell you first hand, that Dolly is one of the nicest most genuine people I have ever met. Money well spent for a very good cause!

Back to work. I always liked going to machine tool auctions and never missed one that had drilling or tapping machines. I accumulated quite an inventory of used machines and began advertising in national machine tool magazines. People were contacting me from all over the world. As I mentioned earlier, tapping is a science unto itself. Most competitors and tapping machine manufacturers just sold the machine or like Snow the machine and tooling. When I built a machine for you, it was turn key ready to go. I not only made the simplest most reliable tooling, but I also knew the proper tap for the application and the proper cutting oil and speeds and feeds. Customers loved the fact that I took all the guesswork out of tapping. The biggest bonus was that the machine was a one time sale, but the taps were perishable and SF Supply would have a new customer every time I sold a machine.

One of the more interesting auctions was earlier in 1974. I had just split with my partner. The auction was a company in Santa Maria that had been manufacturing motorized surf boards. There were some Snow Tapping machines listed, so I went to it. Ed Iskenderian was there. He also loved auctions. I ended up buying the machines that I originally went for. They, then began auctioning off the motorized surf boards. They had 1,200 of them in boxes. They had originally sold for $1,200 each. They were actually quite well-made, they had an inboard motor with a hatch cover and they had a magnetic switch that plugged into the board and a cord attached that went around your waist. If you fell off, the magnetic switch would pull out and shut off the engine. They also had a throttle that you could operate with your toe. But, at $1,200 a piece, it's no wonder they went bankrupt. It was just too expensive for most kids. So, when they began the auction they were a half a dozen kids there. They were the first bidders. The first ones went for $600 each, and then they dropped to about $450 each. Soon, they were out of teenage boys and they announced that it's going to take forever to auction 1,200 surfboards. From now on, you're bidding on a minimum of 10 surfboards each time. The price dropped to $300 each, now I'm starting to get tempted, but I said to myself no way are you buying. What are you going to do with motorized surfboards? The price dropped to $150 each, I said no way I'm not going to buy surfboards the price drop $100 each. Finally, the price got down to $75 each, my hand went up, I now owned 10 motorized surfboards. After I picked up the surfboards, I strapped one to the top of my station wagon out of the carton. I routinely called on other small factory owners like myself, and when I was talking to them they would say what the hell is that? I told them they were motorized surfboards, and I was selling them for $300 each to an entrepreneurial shop owner. They could recognize a bargain when they saw it. I sold all 10 surfboards in a week!

A few weeks later, I stopped by to see my old friend Ed Eskandarian, and said to him I haven't seen you since the auction. He said to me, yeah, did you buy any of those damn surfboards? I said, I sure did. He said, I did too and I don't know what the hell to do with them I paid $75 a piece and they are taking up space in my factory. I said if you want to sell them Ed, I will buy them from you for $75 a piece. He sold them to me, and I sold all of them except one which I kept for my son, so I made a nice little profit on something that I thought I had made a mistake on.

Having come from humble beginnings myself, I have always appreciated a good loyal worker. I had a black lady named Annie Pearl Sims who was one of the best. She lived in South Central Los Angeles. Her only problem was that she had an old car that was constantly breaking down. After a particularly bad spell, where her car broke down about four times in two weeks. I got a call from Annie one morning stating, please don't fire me, my car broke down again. I said Annie, I'm not about to fire you, but if you have to take a bus try to get here tomorrow please. The next morning, Annie showed up and I asked her to get in my car. We went to the local Chevy dealer and I bought her a brand new Chevy Chevette. I said this is your bonus for the next three years, but I bet you won't be late anymore. And she cried, but she became an even more loyal employee. Over the years Annie has called me a few times saying, Wayne if you ever need me to come back to work for you, I am available.

I always tell my employees, I need you as much as you need me.

When you're in business for yourself, one of your biggest problems is dealing with bureaucrats. I think I have become fairly skilled at this. One of the better examples was when I first moved Specialty Tapping to Norwalk Blvd. in the city of Cerritos. I decided I wanted to put up a sign, so I went to a sign maker in Orange County and told him I wanted a 4'x 8' plexiglass sign in orange and black, which was my trademark colors, to put on the side of the building. They quoted me $1400. I thought it was too much money. Someone told me of a sign maker in downtown Los Angeles that was very reasonable. I went to them and they quoted me $300. I ordered a sign, and one Saturday one of my employees and I nailed the sign up on the concrete tilt up building with concrete nails using our forklift. About six months later, a city inspector walked into my front office and asked, did you get a permit to put that sign. I innocently said I didn't know I needed a permit. He said, you most certainly do. So, I went to City Hall and asked to apply for a permit for my sign. They said, well it's a 4'x 8' sign it probably cost you about $1500, so the permit will be $300. I said I only paid $300 for the sign. They said do you have proof? So, I went back and got my receipt and the permit cost $50, but now they're mad at me. The inspector came out and said, I couldn't have an orange and black sign. I said show me where it says that in the ordinance? He couldn't. Then he went up on the roof and measured the height. He says your sign is 18'-6" off the ground, the ordinance says no higher than 18' and he showed me the ordinance. I'm coming back Monday morning and if you haven't lowered it six inches, you will have to remove it. Monday morning he showed up and measures exactly 18' and approved it. I filled up my planter with six inches of dirt!

Another problem I had was that I needed two big air compressors to run my machines. The biggest problem with them was that they were very noisy and they created a lot of heat. They were an especially bad problem in the summertime. So, I went to the city of Cerritos and asked if I could move my air compressors out into the parking lot next to the building. They declined my request saying they didn't meet their noise ordinance. I then asked if I could put a small enclosure out there and put them inside the enclosure. They declined that as well. So, one day I was at an auction and they had a refrigerated truck body off the back of a truck. It even had a license plate on it. I bought it for $100. And, put it next to the building I let it sit there for about six months to see if the city complained. They didn't, so one weekend we moved our compressors into that truck body and ventilated it and left it there until I sold the business in 1990. Another problem solved.

In 1979, I started looking for investments where I could get some tax write offs. I proceeded to make the worst business decision of my life. I started buying condos in Bradenton, Florida, in a new retirement community where my brother was living. The prices compared to California seemed like such a bargain. This was a venture that's still painful. To make a long painful story short, I bought six condos, and over a five year period, I lost $500,000 on them. They were a tax write off for sure!

During that same period in 1980, I bought a 27 acre horse ranch in the city of Lake Elsinore from a doctor for $275,000. The property has a dry creek bed running through it, and during a rainstorm the creek overflowed and flooded the ranch portion where the barns were. There was a house on a hill overlooking the barns and a large new triple wide mobile home. In 1980, interest rates were 17 or 18% on a loan. When the property got flooded the doctor applied for a government loan to rebuild he was approved for a $250,000 loan at 3% interest. When he got the money, he was building a new home in Newport Beach and instead of repairing the damage at the ranch, he used the money to build his new home in Newport. He never expected the government to want to come to the ranch and see the actual repairs. He panicked and heard that if he sold the property, the problem would go away. So, I saw the ad

on a Sunday morning and when I learned of the 3% loan on the property, I told the doctor that I would give him the $275,000 asking price with $25,000 down if I could assume that 3% government loan. I couldn't believe my luck, I was approved to assume the loan and he was off the hook. I wasn't into horses, but I hired a contractor to clean all the sand out of the barns and build a berm along the creek bed. At the time, I was a member of The Glen Eden nudist resort about 8 miles north of the Ranch. They had thousands of large boulders 2 to 4 feet in diameter on their property, and I went to their board meeting and asked if they would like to get rid of some of the boulders. I told them I would take them away free of charge. They were thrilled and approved my offer. I hired a contractor, and took 200 truckloads of boulders and lined the berm so if it flooded again the water wouldn't wash away the sand berm. I leased the ranch to some horse people who turned out to be horrible renters. I got the first and last months rent, and security deposit, and that was it all I ever got from them. It took me six months to a evict them. I put it up for rent a second time. This time, I was more cautious and when a man wanted to lease it, I told him I would take his application pending a credit check. I had a caretaker living there. The next morning, the caretaker called saying a man showed-up and started moving junk cars onto the property telling me that he had just leased it. I took a rifle and jumped in my car and drove to the ranch. I told them they had one hour to get their junk off my property. I waited as they cleared out. My sister was living in Florida and I offered her free rent to come out and replace my caretaker until I figured out what to do with the ranch.

My sister Lois came out from Florida with her live-in boyfriend who was a contractor. After living there a few months, they convinced me that I should build an RV park on the property. So, I proceeded with the permit process and my sister Lois's boyfriend became my contractor, and I built Elsinore Hills RV Park on the property. I was living with my wife Suzanne, who is quite a bit younger than me. She was a senior in college getting a degree in marketing. As I was building the park, she asked me one day if she could do a paper for her school work on the feasibility of my RV Park. I told her I had no objections, so she went to Lake Elsinore and interviewed several RV Park owners who were on the lake. The park I was building was not on the lake, it was across the freeway and I intended it as a long-term RV Park. Back in those days, all RV Parks had a requirement that the maximum stay was no more than six months. However, I knew that this requirement was not closely enforced. After my future wife Suzanne concluded her study, she said, Wayne you're going to do nothing but lose money there, after interviewing all the other owners of Parks. You should stop now. I told her I am not stopping, I'm two thirds of the way finished, I have several hundred thousand dollars invested, it's too late. I finished the park, and six months later, I was making money.

I met my wife Suzanne at the Glenn Eden nudist resort in 1980. We married in 1983 and she became the best business partner I've ever had. She is one of the hardest working people I've ever met, and one of the smartest. We don't always agree on everything, but the fact that we are 25 years apart in age does not diminish the fact that we're far more compatible than I ever was with my first wife. In 1984, Suzanne and I went to a nudist convention at a place called Rawhide Ranch in Wilton, California. We had heard it was up for sale, but I had no interest in it at the time. But, then I started looking around when we were there for the convention. The couple that owned it had a lot of strings attached to the sale. For instance, they had two old men living there, one 83 and one 81 who they said could live there the rest of their life for $35 a month. They also didn't want the name Rawhide Ranch changed for five years. But, the price was half of what I would've expected it to be. So, I offered to buy it for the asking price of $500,000. I had heard that he had put it up for sale before and had buyers, and then he would back out of the deal. So, I told him the only way I would buy it is I would put up a $10,000 nonrefundable deposit and he would get it if I backed out. However, I required him to do the same, and if he backed out I would get his $10,000. We closed escrow on October 1, 1984. It turned out to be a great investment, and since I still had the cutting tool supply business and Specialty Tapping Company, we didn't need a lot of money to live on and we were making a lot of money. Therefore, from 1984 to present we proceeded to turn Rawhide Ranch from a rustic mom and pop 70 acre trailer park to the 250 acre world-class Laguna del Sol Nudist Resort it is today.

CHAPTER 10

I like to attribute my success to a combination of things. Luck definitely played a big part. Two mentors along the way. Beginning with Mr. Maze when I was a teenager and Frank Klause when I was in my 30s. Both believed in me and gave me that hand up when I really needed it. Another element was my dedication to the job at hand and willingness to go out of my way to help others. The forth element was being able to think outside the box and come up with truly innovative ideas.

A good example of just being a good guy and helping someone out, paid off many times over. In the early days of Specialty Tapping, I was working by myself in the factory on a Saturday morning, I had the big overhead door open and a man walked in. He introduced himself as the owner of Master Fence Company in La Habra. He told me he had a new idea for a better and faster way of attaching a chain link fence to the post. The old way was a carriage bolt and nut. His new way required a double headed aluminum rivet, about half the size of spool for thread. He had a blue print and asked if I could make him ten prototype pieces. I told him I'm in the drilling and tapping business, but he looked frustrated that he couldn't get his prototypes made. I said, well let's see if I have a bar of aluminum around, and I will make them myself. I found some and about an hour later, I handed him his prototypes. He tried to pay me and I said I'll tell you what it's lunch time, I'll let you buy lunch. He did and we parted ways. About a month later, he called and said hey my idea worked, now I need 10,000 of the rivets. I said that's not what I do, but I'll see if I can find

a screw machine shop to make them for you. He said I don't have time to mess around, you just get them and add 20% for your trouble. So I did. A month later, he called and said I need 100,000 this time just get them and add 20%. This time, I found a company on Long Island, New York, that could cold head them for one third the cost of a screw machine. I passed the savings through, (I never get greedy.) For over twenty years I received orders from Master Fence for two to three hundred thousand a year for those rivets. I probably made over $150,000 over the years, just because I was a good guy, and took the trouble to make ten rivets.

Another lucrative success was when Hewlett-Packard came out with the first calculator watch. A man came to me with a tapping problem. He had the contract to make the backs for the watch. It was a stainless steel plate 50 thousandths of an inch thick, and H.P. had designed four screw caps in it for accessing the four flat batteries required. Each cap was .500 inches in diameter. Normally, a half inch diameter tap or screw has twenty threads per inch. The problem the engineers encountered was with the plate being so thin, one thread was the same width as the plate. To solve their problem, they had a thin screw with 100 threads per inch. The man that came to me had made the prototype order and when he tried to tap them, had scrapped over 90% of them. So he came to me for my expertise. I quickly analyzed what the problems were and told him, I could do better but not guarantee 100% success. I quoted 50 cents a hole or $2 per plate he was desperate and gave me the order. I scrapped about 10%.

This is one of the aluminum rivets that I had made for Master Fence Co. By the hundreds of thousands over a period of 20 years all because I was willing to accommodate the owner by going out of my way to machine the ten original prototypes for him.

One of the Hewlett-Packard calculator watch backs, the jig I made at 3 a.m., so that I could stack them and tap 20 at a time. Also shown are two of the taps I used to show how fine 100 threads to the inch is and if you look closely, I ground away most of the threads making the process much faster with zero defects.

He was thrilled. The next week he brought me an order for 10,000. That's $20,000. There were two problems. Because the plates were so thin that you could easily strip the threads out while tapping by putting too much down pressure. The second problem was the 100 threads per inch created a hair like chip because it was stainless and the chip, would cling to the tap. After you cut the threads, you then have to reverse the rotation and back it out of the tapped hole. When this happened, the hair like chip clinging to the tap would wedge between the newly cut threads and the tap, and tear out the new threads ruining the parts.

I went to bed dreaming about my new challenge. At three in the morning, I got up and went to work. I had an epiphany I made a jig where I could stack 20 plates on top of one another. Now I was not tapping 20 thin plates, I was essentially tapping one block, one inch thick. Problem number one solved. Next, I ground away all the threads on the tap after the last four full threads. Taps are routinely made with several inches of threads on them, so that they can be cut off and resharpened so that they can be used again-and-again. In this case, a tap

with two inches of threads on it would require it to make two hundred useless revolutions to clear the work piece being tapped. By removing all but four of the threads, the tap it now is finished with the cycle after only four revolutions. Much faster and cost effective.

Next, I mounted and aligned my new jig on the tapping machine with a special quick disconnect holder for the tap. Now, the moment of truth. I started tapping the first hole on twenty stacked plates, when I got all the way through instead of reversing the machine to back the tap back through, I stopped and released the tap and caught it. This new method eliminated ruined parts by dragging the chip back through the tapped holes screwing the tap back through. The big bonus was that production doubled because reversing the tap to extract it took just as long as when it was going forward, actually cutting the threads. I then wiped the tap clean and repeated the process over-and-over. I tapped all 10,000 at night by myself in a week with zero defects. I had made $20,000 in a week. I ended up tapping over 200,000 of these plates over a one year period always doing them myself at night, so no one could steal my simple solution.

CHAPTER 11

From the time we bought the new property in Sacramento in 1984 until 1990, life got hectic. We now were running four very diverse businesses simultaneously. My bread and butter business that started it all, Specialty Tapping, our now very successful business SF Supply, our RV Park in Lake Elsinore which we developed mostly because my sister suggested building it; plus, we couldn't figure out what else to do with it. There was nothing glamorous or outstanding about it, but it was trouble-free with my sister and boyfriend running it, plus it was profitable. My sister Lois had worked at Specialty Tapping while I was building the RV Park. Once it was finished, she quit coming all the way to Cerritos to work at the factory and managed the RV Park and lived in the house we owned.

Lois was ambitious, not to mention she was one of my best workers at Specialty Tapping. We were very busy, so I moved a tapping machine out to the RV Park and Lois would run it Tapping parts in her spare time, on a piece work basis. She even changed her own tools. She made more money on piece work in her spare time, than most of my full-time employees at the factory.

Adding the fourth business, Rawhide Ranch in Sacramento in 1984, I was forced to delegate. My factory manager Jim was very good and a very dedicated hard worker. I relied more on him for the day-to-day operations. I still did the design and development of the new machines. But, my new passion and love was developing Rawhide Ranch.

When I joined Glen Eden Sun Club, south of Corona in 1969 with my first wife, it totally changed my life. I was a general foreman at Kaynar then, and had a pick-up truck with a cab over camper. I wanted to make more use of it, but even back then, on busy weekends unless you made reservations, it was almost impossible to find a place to camp. It was hard for me to plan a week in advance, let alone months. I now had a eleven year old daughter and two sons, nine and six. I saw the founders of Glen Eden on television. They were promoting National Nude Weekend. They were literally preaching the advantages of nudism like it was a religion. I talked my ex into going out to check out this mysterious thing called nudism. We left the kids at home not knowing what to expect. Was it a cult? Would we be exposed to orgies? We were very nervous like I'm sure most people who experience a nudist resort for the very first time. When we arrived at the front gate, we were welcomed by someone and showed us where to park. We went into the office which was a cluttered old trailer. Ray Connett, the man I'd seen on TV sat us down for an interview. I liken it more like a third degree, like a cop would do to a prisoner. After the interview, he said, if you want to take a tour on a golf cart, you will have to remove your clothes now. We almost left, but we bravely persevered. A very nice couple who you would never expect to be nudists took us on the tour. It was a surprisingly nice place with two swimming pools, tennis and volleyball courts, horse shoes, and you name it. To our surprise, there were hundreds of very normal looking people, except no clothes, just having a good time. On our tour, I saw dozens of RV campsites. I said, I didn't know you had camping? How far in advance do you need to reserve one? They said on a busy weekend, you had better get here early on a holiday weekend or you might not get one! That alone sold me. We stayed the day and had dinner with two very nice couples. By the time we left, we had made friends with more people than we had in a year in the textile world. I was hooked! I have said many times since, the nudity will keep you going for a month, the people you meet will keep you a nudist forever.

I got divorced from my first wife in 1971. A year after we married, I had felt it was a mistake, but by that time I had a daughter and I didn't want my kids to suffer through a divorce like I did. But, without birth control, before I knew it I had three kids. In 1971, my ex and I went to a party. There were several older single women there. I talked to several of them, and they all had a similar story after their kids were grown. Their husbands had dumped them. They all said now, I'm over the hill and no one wants me. They were bitter. This was exactly what I was planning. I thought I'm not doing my wife any favors by prolonging the inevitable. She's still attractive why not make both our lives better by correcting our mistake sooner rather than later.

So for the remainder of the 1970s, I was single dating many women mostly 10 to 15 years younger than me. I always looked way younger than I was. I used to hate it, but now I was loving it. In 1979, I was at Glen Eden at the pool and I became friends with two sisters in their teens. The oldest, Suzanne, had just started college. We socialized for almost a year and I became more attracted to Suzanne the better I got to know her. She was extremely smart, attractive, very knowledgeable on world events. She then, as now has a lust for life second to none. But, the barrier that was hard to get over was she was 25 years younger than me. After being around her for a year, the attraction was too strong and fortunately it was mutual. We started dating and now almost 40 years later, I think we made the right decision.

Now, back to Rawhide Ranch, our own Nudist Resort. I often think back to that first day as a nudist in 1969. I always felt that the founders of Glen Eden were going about it all wrong. Nudism isn't a religion it's a form of recreation! I knew how nervous I was approaching the gate. First impressions are important. So, when you approach the gate of what now we call Laguna del Sol clothing optional resort (Rawhide Ranch) you get the impression that you're approaching a country club. Over a period of thirty five years, and millions of dollars, we have created one of the premier nudist resorts in the world. We now have 1,900 members, four swimming pools, three hot tubs, tennis, pickle ball courts and an archery range; with 50 employees, a beautiful restaurant and night club.

Nothing in life ever stays perfect. In 1987, we started to have some storm clouds on the horizon. My key employee Jim, my plant manager bought a house 10 miles south of Corona, 50 miles from Specialty Tapping. A year later Jim started having an affair with my secretary, and at the same time, my sister Lois split-up with her long time live-in boyfriend, and decided to move back to Florida. Jim being newly divorced and needing a place to live offered to manage the Park in exchange for free rent in the house Lois vacated. Now, Jim was the key employee in two of my businesses.

By 1989, my secretary became impossible. She felt because she was Jim's girlfriend she was above being criticized. Finally, she did something that was the last straw, and I fired her. Jim came storming into my office a few minutes later and quit. So, on the same day I lost my secretary, plant manager and RV park manager. Besides these problems workman's comp claims were rising and attorneys had discovered repetitive motion injuries were a lucrative and unprovable new injury claim. I foresaw Specialty Tapping as a prime target for these claims. It was time to go down a new fork in the road.

CHAPTER 12

The timing was good for selling Elsinore Hills RV Park, and within a week I got an offer from some developers. They offered a down payment of 25% if I would finance the balance for ten years interest only. They were willing to pay 10% interest, so I quickly agreed. One problem solved. Now what to do with Specialty Tapping? It was a cash generating machine, but without Jim, it would require me to run it. I also had to consider the fate of all my loyal employees. I owed it to them to find the right person who could successfully take the reigns.

My wife and I had met a very nice young couple at our Resort in Sacramento. We went to Laguna del Sol a few weeks after my foreman left. As luck would have it, they were also there. They were a very attractive couple with two young children. Omar had a BMW repair shop near Lake Tahoe. We visited with Omar and Robyn at the pool. Omar stated he was thinking of selling his business and moving to San Diego. They didn't like the snow. A light bulb went off. I told him about my manager leaving and was thinking of selling Specialty Tapping. I asked if he was interested. He was, but he knew nothing about the business. I knew he was ambitious and bright and his mechanical background was a good foundation.

I offered to hire him and pay him a salary for six months while he was learning and deciding if he was suited to the job. For many years I was ahead of my time and Specialty Tapping worked four ten hour days so everyone except those working overtime got three days off every week. So, Omar and Robyn made the move to San Diego. I wanted this to work so bad that we even let Omar stay in a room in our house for the three weeknights he was working.

I always prided myself on being a good judge of character, but I missed some signals on Omar. I noticed he was very cheap, never offering to pay for his food while staying with us. He was smart and a fast learner. When the June 1st deadline came, Omar agreed to purchase S.T. He was supposed to put down $250,000 and at the last minute, he announced he only had $125,000. He asked if I would I accept a second trust deed on the new home he had just purchased. At this point, I had a lot invested and agreed to accept the note. I later found that was Omar's M.O. constantly reneging on promises. I intentionally made the contract for repayment of the agreed on purchase price very flexible. I knew income could vary wildly and I only wanted to get what was fairly owed to me.

Well, my worries about the income was unfounded because it flourished. I owned the building, so I rented the factory area to Omar and his new business and I stayed in the front office running my supply business. Back when we first agreed, and I hired Omar, I needed a new secretary, and knowing that if it worked out we would want separate secretaries. So I hired two. One of the girls I hired was a young girl (I think she was 20 years old then) her name was Wendy. The other wasn't so memorable. But, in the six month trial period, I came to find out that Wendy was a keeper. She was smart, dedicated loyal and was head and shoulders better than any secretary I ever had. So ,when Omar officially took the reigns of S.T. I made sure Wendy was on my payroll. In many respects she is just like my wife. As a matter of fact, they were both born on the same day, but my wife is eight years older. They are still good friends and we usually have lunch to celebrate their mutual birthdays. Things went well the first year, then Omar started having an affair and ended up in divorce.

In June of 1992, my wife and I went for a two week vacation to England. The day we returned, I went to my office and was going through my mail and there was a letter from Omar's lawyer, stating that Omar felt that he had been cheated and he either wanted his $250,000 back, or reduce the price to 25% of the original agreement. I was shocked, but I couldn't understand why he thought that. Because of my agreement, I got a monthly report on the business and he was doing even better than I expected. Omar walked by my office and I called him in and said, I had no idea you felt this way. Why didn't you come to me instead of involving a lawyer? He said, I thought it was better to do it this way. I said of course, I would give you back your money and we can go our separate ways. A few hours later Omar walked in with the buy-back contract. I said it's not that simple, I have to take an inventory of equipment and have my lawyer look it over. Omar left the premises, so I decided to check-out the factory and equipment. I hadn't been in the factory for several weeks because I was on vacation. I was shocked, half my machines were gone and there were only three employees working, not 18 or 20.

I immediately went into action. My brother-in-law was a cop. I asked if he could tail Omar, so I could find out what he was up to. I told him I would let him know when Omar returns. I then called my attorney. My brother-in-law followed Omar that afternoon when he left S.T., and two miles from S.T., he found Omar's new company called Advanced Tapping with my missing machines, along with the missing employees. OMAR WAS A CROOK!

It turned out his attorney and CPA were also crooks. The CPA would get a new client, typically someone who had just bought a mom and pop business like a car wash or liquor store. Many are seller financed and the couple expect to live out their retirement on the monthly payments. Then, along come these two scum who tell the people who buy the business, I can get the amount you owe greatly reduced for a percentage. Most of the sellers don't have the money to fight a lawsuit, so they agree to the new terms.

This time they got the wrong guy. I spent $250,000 to beat Omar, and the leach attorney. Not only did it cost Omar plenty, he ended up stiffing the attorney. The best part is, it bankrupted the attorney. I won and got most of the money owed, plus I got a lot of the machinery, which I ended up auctioning off.

One side note: All those employees whose jobs I was trying to protect ended up quitting within a year anyway, because Omar was such a cheap horrible person. With the factory empty, and my supply company not needing all that space, I sold my coveted building in 1992. I'd come to a new fork in the road of life.

CHAPTER 13

As if I didn't have enough problems dealing with Omar, the two guys I sold the RV Park to in Lake Elsinore started having financial problems. They at least were honorable men. When they bought the RV Park in 1990, there was a real estate boom and they were over optimistic. They not only bought the RV Park, they bought several hundred acres around the park. Unfortunately for them, the Park was the only income producing parcel they bought. When I sold them the Park, it was full of good tenants. When they started getting in trouble, instead of maintaining the park by spending money repairing things, they used the money to service their debt. They finally gave-up, and deeded it back to me, and I tore up their trust deed. When I got the park back in 1992, occupancy had fallen to 50%. The one good thing that happened was they had hired a young man named Chuck from North Dakota as their manager. He could do plumbing, and electric, an all round handyman. So, I went back to my tried and true formula. I spent about $35,000 upgrading everything that I saw wrong and within six months, we had it full and back in the black. So since it was now trouble free, we decided to keep it.

Now, what to do with my supply business since we had the industrial building in escrow? Real estate prices had dropped since 1990, so I didn't make the killing I could have, but we got a fair price. The advantage was there were a lot of bargains on the market. We ended up buying Westminster Executive Offices near the 405 freeway at Beach Blvd in Westminster. My great secretary Wendy and I moved in before escrow closed in 1992. The whole business of SF Supply fit in one room, and since we took all orders by fax or phone, and either I would deliver locally, or we shipped UPS. We were back in business with the additional business of managers of our new business Westminster Executive Offices. Like most businesses that aren't doing well as this one was, I began to analyze what I needed to do to fill it up. We got free rent while waiting for escrow to close in exchange for managing the day-to-day problems. In the 30 day period, I replaced about a half dozen light bulbs in the hallways. I immediately noticed the wall sconces were metal and the bulbs were confined plus they made the hallways very dark. The first thing I did was replace the hallway lighting with nice bright fluorescent fixtures. The tenants had also told me that they had a lot problems with the roof leaking, so I had them put a clause in the escrow papers that they were responsible for the roof for two years. I then had a sign company make a Marquee sign near the street so tenants could advertise their business. One of my early on new tenants was Cruise America. They were just getting started and rented a 200 square foot office. They weren't there long. They soon out grew us. Wendy was the office manager and pretty much ran SF Supply. I valued Wendy so much that on her Birthday one year gave her a new Chevy Camaro as a company car. The roof leaks did appear and the sellers finally relented on put on a new roof. And guess what? A month later we had a big rain and it leaked. I went up on the roof myself and I found the problem in about ten minutes. I can't believe in the buildings 20 years in existence no one noticed that they had only three two inch diameter drains to handle the runoff for a 8,000 square foot roof. Every flat roof I've ever been on, also had scuppers. These are cutouts at the edge of the roof about two inches above the roof. These are safety valves in case your drains clog. In the case of this roof, they would have been needed for any heavy rain. They were lucky the roof hadn't collapsed. It had been filling up and leaking behind the coved edge of the tar paper. For $600 I had installed three scuppers and a chronic 20 year old problem was solved forever.

We stayed there for six years and I sold it mainly because I was now over 60 years old and didn't want to be fixing toilets anymore. Besides that, Wendy had gotten married and had a baby boy, was pregnant again, and I felt I was asking too much of her. So, I sold Westminster Executive Offices in 1998, and rented an office for SF Supply. But, as I got older I was losing my contacts in the aerospace industry, plus I was no longer building tapping machines for new customers, and thereby creating new tap customers. Wendy decided to become a stay at home mom in 2000, and without Wendy, I decided to sell out. I sold the business back to the tap manufacturer OSG in 2000. I had reached another fork in the road of life.

CHAPTER 14

Now down to two businesses to run, for the first time in years we finally had free time to travel and enjoy the fruits of our efforts. The RV Park in Lake Elsinore was running the best it ever did, thanks to the other short-term owners acquiring Chuck. Laguna del Sol kept getting better and better and the membership was steadily growing. It was busy and fun in the season, but slowed down to a leisurely pace in the three winter months. In the three winter months the costs exceeded the income and we would have to put money into the business. I never liked to put back, so I thought and thought of how to increase winter revenue. In our business weather is everything, and as good as I think I am, I'm not God!

It was time for me to think out of the box again. We have a lot of vacant land and I noticed we had five people storing their trailers in our storage, but storage hadn't been growing. We started a new pull out service. If your trailer was in storage and you wanted to use it, all you had to do is call the office and one of our employees would pull it out of storage and put it on your favorite camp site, and we would return it to storage when you were ready to leave for home. We also would empty the holding tank for a slight extra charge. This service became a resounding success and the number of RVs in storage has grown from five in 1996 to over 300 today. Many of our members buy a new trailer and put it in our storage and never buy a tow vehicle. This idea was a win-win for everyone. We didn't have to raise prices to keep from losing money and we obviously provided a very valuable needed service. Plus, not only

did it help our bottom line, but we shared our success with our employees increasing our contribution to their retirement plan. It goes back to my mantra for success... RECOGNIZE A NEED AND FILL THE NEED!

Nudist camps began to appear in remote locations in more tolerant states back in the 1930s, and because of the stigma attached back then, they were perceived as cult-like. Most were started by like minded people as co-ops. Many of those are still in existence today.

Many of the old school nudists who belong to these rustic campgrounds complain that nudism is dying. Rustic campgrounds are dying whether nude or not. The co-ops are not business oriented they don't have any incentive to improve or grow. In fact, most of them shun upgrades. That could raise the membership costs. The ones that are flourishing are the ones that are constantly improving and adding amenities when recognizing the need. I have always preached that to my fellow resort owners.

A good example of a great model for business that started out very successful, but never changed their model when competitors came along with a better model was The Club Med organization. They were the first all inclusive vacation destination resorts. They had great locations and were a fun place to go. I used to go all the time to the ones in Tahiti, Martinique, Bahamas and Cancun. They were low end budget oriented. They didn't have AC and the liquor was box wine and beer. Competition seized on their success and went upscale including premium liquor and AC. Places like Sandals and Beaches, soon put them out of business.

I have always said, the best way to make nudism or any other business grow is, if someone sees that you have a good business model, others will try to duplicate what you're doing.

One of my members and a friend of mine was a Vice President of a big bank that got acquired by an even bigger bank. He got a big golden parachute buyout. So, he told me he wanted to start his own nudist resort. He was looking in Southern California, and I wasn't worried about competition. I even went with him to look a several properties. We went to a property off Interstate 8 and looked at an old 1,000 trails campground. It was big 500 acres. The problem was, it was in a remote location with no phone service or local television. It needed a lot of work, but it had a 10,000 square foot main building and two nice swimming pools. Well, my friend bought it and it was almost an overnight success. I was happy to see the industry growing. He had a little luck as well as he was soon able to get satellite TV and radio, so he was no longer totally isolated. This was I believe 1995.

In 2006, he contacted me and said he had found this great old resort near Tucson, Arizona that was for sale, and he thought it would make a great nudist resort. I flew over and we had a third friend from Florida who owned a nudist resort near Tampa fly in as well.

I was impressed with the property. It wasn't isolated at all. It had been a going business for 160 years. A lot of history. It was only 30 acres, but the attractive thing is, it was already approved to build 116 condos. My friends Dave and Joe wanted to make an offer on it, as the owner was from Chicago and was anxious to sell. He proposed

we be three equal partners (actually six because we were all married). I said to them do you two have any idea what we're in for? Even though it was a going business as a destination resort with all the amenities and was complete with silverware for the restaurant and linens for the fourteen hotel rooms, we are literally starting a brand new business since the nudist industry is completely different. I said to my two future partners. Do you realize what you're getting into? Are you prepared to put $10,000 a month each in the first year and if we're lucky maybe only $5,000 a month the second year and maybe break even by the third?

I said besides that, I'm 70 years old. They said it won't be that bad. We will do all the work, we want you on board because of your money and reputation.

Well, we bought Mira Vista Resort on May 1st, 2006 as partners and friends. I was right on with my estimate of $10,000 each for the first year. I was wrong about the second year. It cost us $7,000 a month each. The third year was 2009 when the economy really went to hell. I was fortunate that I had cash and a good income stream from my other businesses.

Joe was the first to fall by the wayside. The financial strain was too much. By 2009, we had already had designs and permits for the first 17 condos. Before we could even begin building, we had to bring city water and sewer onto the property, from almost a mile away. Plus, we had to put in curb and gutter and paved roads. The property had been on well and septic with dirt roads. We were talking big bucks!

Dave and I bought Joe and his Wife's share equally. We were now 50-50 partners.

Everyone has a different idea of the best way to run a business, even husbands and wives.

The three of us always thought differently, but we agreed early on that we would vote. I was almost always two against one, but it worked and we managed to remain friends. Once we bought out Joe, the path foreword got more difficult. My vision was a first class high-end resort that would be the envy of the nudist world. Dave's vision was more a beer hall atmosphere. Well, our strained relationship led to Suzanne and I buying Dave and Helen out in late 2009. The saddest thing about this partnership is, I genuinely liked my partners. We are not enemies now, but we are not the close friends we were before .The moral of the story is never go into business with friends.

What did we get ourselves into? For sure, we were starting down a new fork in the road of life!

CHAPTER 15

Ahead of Suzanne and I lay the biggest challenge of our lives. At 74 years old and coming from meager beginnings, I was always cautious. I took risks, but I would never risk more than about 10% of my net worth. That way, if I failed I might have a temporary setback, but I wouldn't lose everything.

In 2010, we had just bought out our partners and we still owed $2,500,000 to the people we all had originally purchased the property from and we were paying 8% interest. We had badly depleted our savings buying out our partners. We were sitting on a set of approved plans and a permit to put in all the infrastructure of the first 17 condos. Unfortunately, in 2010 the economy was bad and to further sour the market there were several ambitious people in the nudist industry with big dreams and no money that had gotten an option on a beautiful piece of Caribbean beach property, and had a beautiful brochure made up touting this new nudist resort. They were taking deposits for this dream. Unfortunately, none of them ever followed through and the deposits disappeared.

So, here we are with our dream property in the Arizona desert. We did have a good track record owning Laguna del Sol for 25 years. We didn't want to even start the project without having at least 50% of the 17 units pre-sold. We had three solid buyers: one couple who were good friends, a couple who had a place at Laguna del Sol and a newly retired couple from Kansas. The owner of Bare Necessities, a very prestigious and respected clothing optional cruise agency who chartered whole cruise ships that held 3,000 passengers had been to Mira Vista several times and loved it. Her clientele were my target customers, they were nudists and had money. I offered her a condo at a substantial discount and she was on board. So, things were looking brighter. My partners out voted me on which phase to start first, so that's why building two was permitted first. There were ten total phases. I wanted to start with what I perceived to be the best group of 17 buildings, five and six near the entrance that I thought had the best views. The partners outvoted me and picked building two for practicality. It was furthest from the entrance and they felt after it was completed, the residents wouldn't be disturbed by future construction. Because of this, many prospective buyers were reluctant to pick a unit in building two. I had to get creative. I believed in the project and knew that whoever bought at $199,000 was getting a real bargain and prices would go up on future phases. So, I started offering to take any condos purchased in building two during preconstruction in trade on a future condo for the original price. To further spur sales, we started offering to include a 10 year membership for a couple at Mira Vista Resort which is a separate entity.

This didn't cost us any money out of pocket. Contractors were desperate for work in 2010 and prices would never be better. We had the elements in place to move forward. Well, all of the elements except the biggest one of all MONEY! We needed $5,000,000 and banks weren't loaning to anyone, let alone a risky condo venture at a nudist resort!

I first was able to obtain a $3,000,000 loan against our well established Laguna del Sol Resort which was free and clear with 5% interest. I first paid off the original $2,500,000loan that we were paying 8% interest on so the extra $500,000 cost us nothing, because of the savings on interest. Second we raided our retirement accounts by setting up a legal Entrepreneur Rollover Stock Ownership Plan (ERSOP) which allows you to use your retirement money for ventures such as this. We were still over $2,000,000 short. I came up with a new idea. We had lots of real estate that was paid for, so I was going to offer a first trust deed on a piece of property in exchange for a loan of at least $100,000 for one, two, or three years at 5, 5.5, or 6% respective to the length of the loan. I first offered it to all my poker buddies, who I have been playing poker with for over 25 years. Keep in mind, you couldn't get 1% at a bank in 2010. They all shrugged and said not interested. Suzanne said, I guess we have to give up. I said let's try one last thing.

We have electronic newsletters at both resorts that reach about 2,500 people. I sent out the same offer to them. Within three weeks, I had all the money I needed and was turning people down. One of my members who I had only known for a few years said, Wayne I have $500,000 I can lend you. What are the terms? I told him, this is while we were at the gym working out. He said I don't think so . I said, well how much interest do you want. He said, oh that's not what I meant. I can't get 1% at the bank, I would feel guilty getting that much from you. How about giving me 3% interest and a lifetime membership. He was 70 at the time! I said, I have three properties worth over $1,000,000 you can pick which one you want a trust deed on. He said, naw your signature on a note is good enough for me! My friends, if this true testimonial doesn't convince you that nudists are the greatest people you will ever encounter, then nothing will.

We went to work putting in all the infrastructure and built the first 17 condos. We have since built two more phases for a total of 55 condos ,with the next phase of 10 more almost ready to start. As a side note those who initially bought for $199,000 only one took me up on the trade-in option, and I doubt if any one else will, as the new ones start at $269,900.We have since paid everyone off, including the bank loans, and our retirement fund.

I believe the 10 year period from 2009 through 2019 was the most challenging of our lives. The payback is the extreme pride in our accomplishments at both Laguna del Sol and Mira Vista.

When we attend an event at either reesort, it is so rewarding to watch so many people getting along so well and having so much fun. There is not a weekend that passes at either of our resorts that more than one couple will stop by our table and say thank you so much for creating such a wonderful place. We have received letters from couples saying how discovering Laguna del Sol or Mira Vista has totally changed their life for the better. Even my sister Lois, who was very reluctant to even visit Laguna del Sol to see her brothers newest venture, finally stopped by on a vacation for a tour and ended up living there and loving it, making more friends and knowing more people than me. She died four years ago at the resort. I haven't completed my road of life yet and if luck is with me I will continue my quest to complete Mira Vista and continue to improve Laguna del Sol.

I have often looked back over my life's journey to see if I would change anything. I don't think I would. It's been a challenge and an adventure. I have a great sense of accomplishment and feel that I have changed many people's lives for the better.

Unless I drive over a cliff, look for an update on my road through life in about twenty years, because I'm not finished yet!

— Wayne Schell

FAVORITE PHOTOS

This is the hill my Dad was driving an ice truck down the day I was born.
The brakes went out and he ended up in the hospital next to my mom and me.

This picture from left to right. The little guy on the left is me at fourteen. The next two on each side of my brother are my cousins visiting from Pennsylvania. The guy in the middle is my brother Dick. The guy on the right is my neighbor Jim Lucas who was actually a year younger than me, but he was 6 feet 6 inches tall when he was fifteen.

This was the view from my front porch of the old house we lived in. It's a mountain of slag from the coal mine that was across the road from our house.

The other photo is my Dad, my brother and four sisters. The only two left alive is me and my youngest sister Sue, who is ten years younger than me.

LES-BUZZ BALLROOM and ROLLER RINK —
Central Illinois' Gayest Spot

Located on U. S. Route 6 on west side of Spring Valley, Illinois. Featuring roller skating nitely except Mon. and Sat. (which are private party nites) plus name bands twice monthly. Upper left photo shows stage of colored fiberglass illuminated with neon lights. Upper right photo shows the Les-Buzz sound wagon, equipped with hi-fi tape recorder-amplifier and speaker mounted in grill. Sign on top of car lights up for night advertising and features interchangeable letters to announce coming attractions.

The Les-Buzz Ballroom where the big bands played.

A playbill for the Les-Buzz Ballroom.

Louis Armstrong himself with Buzz Verucci the week I took him to his room at the hotel Kaskaskia

Construction of the interstate highway test road when I worked in the gravel pit.

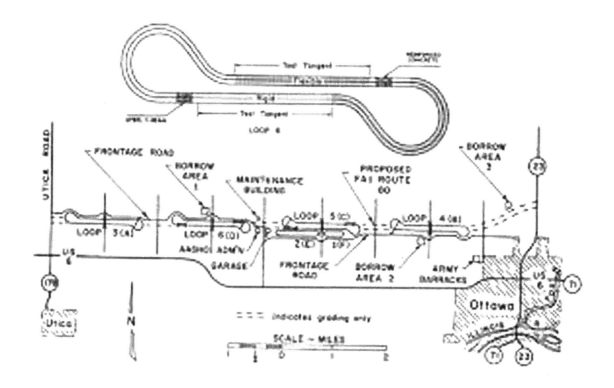

Suzanne and Wayne attending their niece Kelly's wedding in Chicago in 2019.

These two nieces and nephew sitting on Suzanne's lap 30 years ago are now the parents of the two Grand-nieces and Grand-nephews sitting with Suzanne on the picture below.

The Hewlett Packard calculator watches were over $3,000 when they first came out. When the prices dropped to about $300, I bought one. I was wearing it in 1976 when I won the Mr. Nude USA Contest, and the other contestants threw me into a swimming pool in celebration and ruined it.

Suzanne with our grandnephews and grandnieces.

My two Grandnieces and Grandnephew love getting in my chair when I'm heading for it. And, of course I have to make a really big deal out of it!

When their parents were that age, they also took great delight in this same prank. Living proof that kids are no different today than they were 30 years ago.

Laguna del Sol Resort, Wilton, Califonia. | *www.lagunadelsol.com*

Mira Vista Resort, Tucson, Arizona | www.miravistaresort.com

At 84 years old, enjoying my next generation mid-engine 2020 C8 Corvette, which I picked-up in Queens, New York, and drove it back to California during the Covid Pandemic.

EPILOGUE

Almost two years have passed since I finished my book. Now at 85, I'm still plugging away just when I'm cruising down a smooth highway life hit us all with probably the roughest stretch of road we will all ever encountered, Covid 19. Timing in life is everything. If Covid would have hit at several points in my life, it could have easily bankrupted me. But again, luck played a prominent role. We had just closed escrow on 12 of the 17 condos we had just completed, allowing us to pay-off our debts and taxes. But, when Covid hit, like everyone, our businesses came to a virtual screeching halt. We sat on the remaining five unsold condos for 1-1/2 years, and Mira Vista in Tucson needed several cash infusions to survive. Fortunately, Laguna del Sol is not only a destination resort, but it's also a mobile home and R/V park with permanent site rentals. Our gross income dropped, but we were still profitable.

I personally went out of my way to patronize and support good local small businesses to help them survive, as I'm sure many of you have as well. As of July 2021, Covid is waning and for those of us businesses that survived, business is booming. The final five unsold condos all sold within weeks back in February 2021. We have broken ground on the next phase of 10 condos with a strong demand of willing buyers. The newest challenge is obtaining contractors and materials at a reasonable cost as well, as getting willing reliable workers to fill the vacancies that Covid created. But, at least we are back on a smooth path forward once again.

One bonus that we are relishing in is, we are getting more new customers at both resorts than ever before. I think the reason is these people either normally travel internationally or cruise, but since neither of those forms of recreation are available, they are vacationing in the U.S. and trying something different.

—Wayne Schell

ABOUT THE AUTHOR

Wayne Schell

This is the place where all good authors tell you something about themselves. How do you embellish on an autobiography when you've just told your life story? With that said, as I referenced in my book, I love to talk and tell stories and make people laugh. When I start to tell someone a story, those who know me will ask. Okay is this story for real or is this one of your jokes? So, I will leave you with a couple examples and hopefully a good laugh.

Three years ago on Christmas Eve morning, I told Suzanne I'm going to be sitting and watching football all day. So I won't feel guilty, I'm going to the gym and to do it right, I'm going to ride my bike. So, I rode my bike the two miles to the gym and worked out. I took a different route home after finishing. There had been a doughnut shop on the corner under renovation for about a month. This Christmas Eve morning, there was a banner that said Grand Opening, Under New Management. I thought, a doughnut sounds good. Then I remembered, I don't have any money with me. Then I recalled that I keep a plastic bag with loose change in it, in my bike pack. I stopped at the donut shop and looked in my change bag and I had $1.25. Since I haven't bought a doughnut in years, I had no idea what a doughnut cost. When I walked in, there were two firemen ahead of me buying two bags of doughnuts for the whole fire station just West of the doughnut shop. I waited patiently for them to finish. Finally one of the clerks asked what I would like. I said first off, how much is a cream filled chocolate doughnut? She said one dollar. I said great I have enough money. I'll have one and proceeded to count out $1 in change. The two firemen looked me up and down in my old gym clothes and saw I was riding a bicycle. They said sir, it's Christmas Eve, we don't want you to spend your last dollar on a doughnut, we'll buy. I said guys thanks, but I assure you I can afford it. They said it makes us feel good that we can help you out on Christmas Eve. I said, if I was driving my Corvette you wouldn't be offering to buy my doughnut. They said, yeah sure, you have a Corvette. A week later, I drove my Corvette and went into the doughnut shop and asked if the firemen had been in yet? They said no, so I said give me whatever they normally buy. I took the two bags of doughnuts to the fire station and one of the firemen was there and I said doughnuts are on me this morning. He said, damn you really do have a Corvette! This is an absolutely true story.

More recently when vaccinations became available for Covid 19, I was one of the first to receive it because of my advanced age. After the second shot, they make you wait for fifteen minutes in case of adverse reactions before leaving. No problems, so I left, but driving home everything was blurry. When I got home, I turned on my TV. I couldn't see it. I immediately called the clinic and said you have a problem. Something is wrong, I can't see and I'm going straight to my doctor when I hang up. They said is this Mr. Schell? I said yes it is. They said don't do that, just come back here and get your glasses. You forgot them!

This was a joke! Have a great road of life yourself.

CPSIA information can be obtained
at www.ICGtesting.com
Printed in the USA
LVHW070150040921
696919LV00003B/7

9 781733 729369